❧ **W9-BSS-642**

"COMPELLING . . . presents Maggie's life in her own simple, direct language, filled with understated eloquence and wisdom." —*Cleveland Plain Dealer*

"SHOULD BE READ BY ALL PARENTS WHO ARE CONCERNED ABOUT EDUCATION AND THEIR CHILDREN'S FUTURE." —Alvin Poussaint, M.D.

"REMARKABLE, ENGROSSING . . . told in a simple but riveting style. —*Atlanta Daily World*

"ELOQUENTLY INSPIRING . . . Maggie's own story is particularly moving because of the honesty of her voice." —*San Diego Tribune*

"A TRIBUTE TO THE THOUSANDS OF UNKNOWN BLACK WOMEN IN AMERICA WHO HAVE BEAT THE ODDS IN REALIZING THE GREAT AMERICAN DREAM." —Mary Hartwood Futrell, President, National Education Association

"POIGNANT." —*Essence*

Maggie's
American Dream

The Life and Times of a Black Family

by
James P. Comer, M.D.

With a Foreword by Charlayne Hunter-Gault

A PLUME BOOK

To my mother and father,
and all our children

PLUME
Published by the Penguin Group
Penguin Books USA Inc., 375 Hudson Street, New York, New York 10014,
U.S.A.
Penguin Books Ltd, 27 Wrights Lane, London W8 5TZ, England
Penguin Books Australia Ltd, Ringwood, Victoria, Australia
Penguin Books Canada Ltd, 10 Alcorn Avenue, Toronto, Ontario, Canada
M4V 3B2
Penguin Books (N.Z.) Ltd, 182–190 Wairau Road, Auckland 10, New Zealand
Penguin Books Ltd, Registered Offices: Harmondsworth, Middlesex,
England

Published by Plume, an imprint of Dutton Signet, a division of Penguin
Books USA Inc.

First Plume Printing, November, 1989

16

Maggie's American Dream previously appeared in an NAL BOOKS edition
published by New American Library and simultaneously in Canada by
The New American Library of Canada Limited (now Penguin Books
Canada Limited).

"I, too, sing America" from *Selected Poems of Langston Hughes,* copyright
1926, by Alfred A. Knopf, Inc. and renewed 1954 by Langston Hughes.
Reprinted by permission of Alfred A. Knopf, Inc.

Original hardcover designed by Leonard Telesca

 REGISTERED TRADEMARK—MARCA REGISTRADA

Library of Congress Cataloging-in-Publication Data
Comer, James P.
  Maggie's American dream: the life and times of a Black family / by
James P. Comer; with a foreword by Charlayne Hunter-Gault.
    p.   cm.
  ISBN 0-453-00588-8
  ISBN 0-452-26318-2 (pbk.)
  1. Comer, Maggie, 1904–   . 2. Afro-Americans—Biography.
3. Afro-American families. 4. Comer, James P.—Family. I. Title.
E185.97.C68C66   1988
973'.0496073022—dc19
[B]   88-15936
                                                                     CIP

Acknowledgments

I would like to thank the many people who helped me write this book. First, and foremost, a very special thanks to my mother, Maggie Comer. Without her care and sharing this book would not have been possible. And for the same reasons, I owe a special thanks to my brothers and sisters— Louise, Norman, and Charles Comer, and Thelma Comer Morris. And a special thanks to my wife, Shirley, and our children, Brian and Dawn Comer, for their interest, support, and valuable comments about the manuscript.

I owe Al Solnit, David Musto, Henry "Skip" Gates, Richard and Valarie Wesley, Tim Shriver, and Julie Cooper a special debt. They encouraged me to write, and to continue writing, this book at times when I had decided that the project was not feasible. My thanks to my editors: Carole Hall, who "found" the story, and LuAnn Walther and John Paine, who helped me tell it. I would like to thank James Boger, Edward Joyner, Muriel Hamilton-Lee, Norris Haynes, and other members of our Child Study Center Team who provided comments and support that made this book possible. I would like to thank all the children, all the parents, and all the past and present professional staffs in New Haven and in other school districts who allowed me to work with them, and to learn from them in a way that helped me to better understand myself, schools, and the place of schools in our society.

Finally, I would like to thank my office support staff, who have worked on this project on and off for almost a decade—Janice Gore, Barbara Johnson, Debbie Weiner, Kathy Stomboli, Shirley Ryan. And a very special thanks to my Administrative Secretary, Ms. Etta Burke, who has lived with the project and done the lion's share of managing most aspects of its production from beginning to end.

CONTENTS

I, too, sing America.

I am the darker brother.
They send me to eat in the kitchen
When company comes,
But I laugh,
And eat well,
And grow strong.

Tomorrow,
I'll sit at the table
When company comes.
Nobody'll dare
Say to me,
"Eat in the kitchen,"
Then.

Besides,
They'll see how beautiful I am
And be ashamed—

I, too, am America.

—Langston Hughes

FOREWORD

When I first talked with Jim Comer about *Maggie's American Dream*, it immediately struck a chord. I thought of writer Alice Walker's work, *In Search of Our Mother's Gardens*, her way of looking back into that rich soil for the answers to how we all endured and prevailed, despite the blighting of so many fruits.

I heard the same chord of recognition during my brief sojourn in South Africa. "Now that you have touched the women," goes a popular saying among anti-apartheid activists, "you have struck a rock . . . you have dislodged a boulder. . . ."

It also resonated in my own life, in a small Georgia town, where the otherwise-limiting aspects of Jim Crow were more than amply overcome by the pillars of my childhood . . . home, school, church . . . separate, but never inferior in terms of the armor-building preparation for life. Women like Jim Comer's mother Maggie were at the rock-solid center of it all.

The small Southern town where I grew up was not that fundamentally different from the Indiana of Jim Comer's childhood. Even though segregation was legally outlawed "up North," Indiana was still a place where blacks had to watch their backs. There, as well as in the South of my childhood, the black community and its institutions were the only places you could take for granted. And that extended to the idea that anybody who saw you misbehaving could administer punishment on the spot—from a tongue-lashing to something more severe, without fear of reprisal from the otherwise-occupied parent.

But *Maggie's American Dream* is also meaningful for me in its story of a strong black man who struggled against the odds to provide both materially and spritually for his family. Jim Comer's father eventually had to leave his home (but not his family) and move out West for his health. Seeking more dignity and self-respect than he could get in the segregated South, my father left us at home and joined the military.

But despite their long absences, these men left their values behind and their good women to take care of those values; and they worked hard at maintaining their own presence in the home. In my father's case, he used to send long, detailed letters about his travels (and travails), and occasional voice recordings telling us how much he missed us, and, most importantly, his expectations for us.

For me, as for Jim Comer, these were expectations of good grades. ("Good grades," he writes, "could save me from a lot of grief, at home and at school.")

I never shall forget my father's visits home—thirty days at a time, usually. One of the first things he wanted to know about after he got home was my grades. Proudly, I would show him my report card. Usually I got A's, but there was an occasional B. If I got all A's, little was said. That was what was expected of me. But if there was a B among the A's, the only thing my father would want to know was why I'd gotten the B.

As much as his expectations fueled my desire to succeed, so too did my mother's hands-on involvement in my schoolwork, as well as in my school. Like Maggie Comer, Althea Hunter was one of those parents who took an active role. She was there when needed. And because of the inferior budgets for black schools in Georgia, she was needed when it came time raise money.

I always got to be the school queen because my mother and grandmother raised the most money. I'll never forget the nervous anticipation as we waited on the night the queen was to be named while my mother counted out the thousands of pennies, nickels, and dimes that she had brought to school wrapped in white linen handkerchiefs. The money was used to buy books and other school supplies that routinely came with the territory in the white schools.

My mother and grandmother and other mothers and grandmothers raised money, but still not enough to spare us from having to use secondhand, often outdated textbooks from the white schools—books that never included black history. But these women and our teachers—also mostly all women—supplied something else that money couldn't buy and the law couldn't limit, and that was a sense of pride in who we were and where we came from and where we were going. As routinely as they continued to raise the pennies, the notion of education as an essential ingredient of my life became part of my thinking.

It never occurred to me that I wouldn't go on to college after high school. Or achieve my goals. I don't recall that we actually ever discussed it in so many words. It was just what queens did. By the same token, it is clear that in Maggie Comer's eyes, her son was a king. As he so lovingly demonstrates throughout the poignant rendering of his mother's oral history and his own recollections, that kind of parental understanding is where self-esteem begins— the stuff needed to propel little black boys and girls (indeed, all children) to their best destinies.

This innate understanding was coupled with a strong sense of historical pride. Every day was black-history day. In my case, in the still-segregated South, it was as if, lacking the power to legally grant us first-class citizenship, our parents and our extended family at school and at church more than made up for it by giving us a first-class sense of our identity.

Sometimes it could be done as casually as when Maggie

Comer first told her young son about slavery—in church after a giggling episode he had shared with his brother while the elderly ladies on the Mothers' bench were singing.

"In self-defense," Comer writes, "I argued that we didn't mean any harm, but that those ladies couldn't sing. 'Why do they allow them to sing?'

"Mom said, 'You ought to show more respect. Some of those ladies were born in slavery!'

" 'Slavery? What's that?'

"There was an ominous pause, and then solemnly she said, 'Slavery is when somebody else owns you and you have to work for them and do everything they tell you. And if you don't they can beat you, sell you, or anything else they want to do to you.'

" 'Who was in slavery?' I asked hesitantly.

" 'All of our people. You had to be strong to make it. That's why we're such strong people now.' "

While it's wonderful to have a work like *Maggie's American Dream* evoke the memories that help explain our successes and our outlook on life, that is far from its only strength. Another value lies in the promise it holds out in an otherwise-despairing outlook found in much of the black community today.

My generation just may have been the last generation to benefit from the institutions that were the instruments for success: the home, the church, the school. To the extent that they still exist, they certainly no longer perform for this generation as they did for us.

And the evidence is there for us all to see. Indeed, much of what we see fuels the growing public debate over what to do about the breakdown of the family, about welfare, about the criminal-justice system, and, in my view, about the most important issue of them all—the education system.

On the streets of New York and other cities as well are children of the age that I was when I was queen, whose mothers have never seen the inside of their children's schools. It is even the case that some of their mothers are not much older than I was when I was queen. These are the children who frighten me almost more than anything else I've seen that is wrong in this society. Not because I fear them, but because they have no light in their eyes— the light that would enable them to see the future. And if they cannot see the future, then there is indeed reason to fear . . . because they *are* our future.

With the same certainty that gave Maggie her dreams for her children, Jim Comer gives us hope that we can turn the light back on.

With elegant simplicity, Comer takes the values of his childhood, the education of his youth, and the experiences of his adult training, and shows a way out of indifference, hand-wringing, despair. This is no academic exercise. I know of no one who has more clearly and more effectively demonstrated the synergy between home and school and who has gotten results even in the poorest communities.

Maggie Comer's son inherited her dream and it is now his own. It is a dream that can make kings and queens of all our children. It should not be a dream deferred. And once you read Jim Comer's book, it need not be. America's weakened families of all races and classes can take courage from this story.

—Charlayne Hunter-Gault
New York, June, 1988

INTRODUCTION

We stood in the doorway of the small Baptist church in Comer, Alabama, and looked out over the graveyard where several generations of my father's family were buried. A few headstones were toppled, some crumbling, some completely obscured by snarled growths of weeds. My cousin Donald gave the Who's Who among the dead: "Grandpa Morgan is over here. He was the pastor of this church. Great-grandma Rebecca is over there," and so on. My son, Brian, and daughter, Dawn, looked on with a kind of academic interest, but I was deeply moved. I thought to myself, "Here lies the history of my family— gone forever."

It was the year of the *Roots* phenomenon, and like many Americans we were motivated to learn more about our family history. To do so we had taken a trip to my father's birthplace and childhood home. From the moment we spotted the roadside sign COMER on U.S. Highway 82, my emotions began to churn. The village of Comer is named after former slave masters of the same name, not my relatives. In the museum in Eufala, to the southeast, there was a picture of one of my relatives posing with a white officer, whom he served during the Civil War. A picture of my great-grandma Rebecca hung on the wall of the gymnasium of the Rebecca Comer High School in Comer, named in her honor. She was the former slave of John and

later the servant of his son, Braxton Comer, former governor of Alabama. I was curious about her high cheekbones
and light skin. Cousin Donald doubted a blood kin. "The
Comers weren't like that," he said matter-of-factly. "They're
decent people."

I had always heard the same from my father. Dad and
Mom had mentioned several times that when the white
Comers stopped growing cotton, they sold the land to
blacks and whites at the same price while many landown-
ers wouldn't sell to blacks at all, or required that blacks
pay more. Also, they built a modern and well-cared-for
high school for blacks before the days of school integration. Recently I met the former superintendent of schools
of Birmingham, Alabama, who told me that when he had
attempted to integrate that school system, the only white
community leader who openly supported him—"because
it is right and fair"—was Hugh Comer, the governor's
son, my father's childhood friend, and one of the country's leading textile producers then.

Cousin Donald also showed us the old cotton mill—
abandoned and decaying just off the main street in town.
Weeds had overgrown the railroad tracks that once took
cars carrying cotton to and from the mill. The buildings
that once housed the few stores in town were now beyond
repair. The last sale on the rusting gasoline pump in front
of the long-closed Grant Bros. Gen. Mdse. store was $1.23.

We were warmly received by relatives as Donald introduced us as "Uncle Hugh's son and family from up North."
Donald's home was a handsome ranch house, and he was
the principal of the Rebecca Comer High School. His wife
taught at the racially integrated school in Eufala. We visited the well-kept country homes of several white Comers.
We chatted briefly with some of my relatives who worked
for them as gardeners, housekeepers, and the like. Other
relatives live in shanties and survive on government subsi-
dies of one kind or another. Comer is in Barbour County,

one of the poorest in the nation—a victim of industrialization and post-industrialization.

It was my second visit to Comer. I was about six years old the first time. All I can remember from that first visit was the uneasy feeling I experienced when somebody encouraged me to touch a pig's snout. Over the years my father recalled with amusement the time my brother and I came running into the house greatly frightened, exclaiming, "Daddy, Daddy, there's something with great big ears and great big eyes and a great big hump behind it out there. And it's coming this way!" It was a mule hitched to a plow.

Cousin Donald, about my age, remembered that my cap had flown out of the window of the truck as we departed thirty-five years before. He had gotten his first city cap from our visit. But even these trifling remembrances were more than I gained from the graveyard. The graveyard was silent. The more people and places we visited, the more I kept thinking, "These lives—past and present— something complex and important happened here. But it's all gone. This should not be forgotten!"

I wanted to do something about it. But I didn't know what.

That winter we took a vacation in Barbados, and my mother went along, as she often does. I had heard bits and pieces of her story over the years, but I had never thought of my mother's life story as noteworthy in any way. In rearing the five of us, weren't she and Dad simply doing what parents are supposed to do? And besides, Mom was a hard taskmaster, and I was only a few years past the feelings of anger and resentment that she had pushed me so hard. But given my feelings in the graveyard in Comer, it occurred to me to bring my tape recorder along to record her history. My mother wasn't getting any younger, seventy-two at the time.

About six months later I read the transcript, and then showed it to Albert Solnit, my longtime professional mentor. I had decided that if Al saw any value in it, I would continue. And besides, it was only to be a family record. He returned it with a little note attached: "Very rich. Why don't you develop it?"

The next time I visited my mother I took my tape recorder. On and off over the next three to four years I taped Mom's story. Mom had had almost no schooling and survived through her wit, guile, and caution. Thus, she didn't readily show all the cards in her hand, even to her son. But I knew many things about her life from the stories she had told over the years, and I asked her questions about what I knew. In the process of answering, she relaxed and began to tell me more about her life, and eventually began to rejoice in reliving it through the interviews.

As her story emerged, I sensed that what I was hearing was more than a family document; it was an oral history. I showed the manuscript to a screenwriter, Richard Wesley. He was encouraging and said, "What you have is an encapsulation of the black South-to-North movement."

A light went on in my head. Much of my previous thinking and research—particularly as discussed in my first book, *Beyond Black and White*—had dealt with how slavery and a racial caste system had limited the black community's ability to undergo the three generations of development in response to economic changes in the manner of other racial and ethnic groups in America. Most of the immigrants who came in search of the American Dream—the ability to provide well for themselves and their families as valued members of a democratic society—didn't find it in one generation. It usually took two or three. My mother, Maggie, believed that education was the way to achieve her American Dream. When she was denied the opportunity herself, she declared that all her children would be educated. Mom and Dad together gave all five of us the support needed to acquire thirteen college degrees.

This story, then, is my mother's struggle, with my father's help, as well as my own experiences. My experiences—

and those of my siblings—are a window on her life and the life and times of America during the first half of the twentieth century. But there is more.

I have discussed my work in the inner-city schools of New Haven all over the nation. I often contrast my own family experience—five college-educated children of under-educated, low-income parents—with that of friends from the same background who were just as intelligent but whose lives had less desirable outcomes. This points to critical differences that go beyond racial issues alone. Frequently black professionals in the audience tell me that their family stories are very similar. These are black family stories that are not being told by scholars and a media obsessed with "the victims," or worse, "those who are not able or not trying." An understanding of the strategies and strengths of the "survivors" will tell us more about the obstacles and ways around them than an exclusive focus on "the victims."

Recently while on the road discussing my work, I met a friend from many years back, Alice Dunston, the widow of one of my best friends in medical school. She is the principal of a rapidly improving elementary school in one of the lowest-income areas in Newark, New Jersey. I congratulated her and she said—in a warm Southern drawl she has not lost over all these years—"Comer, I care about these kids as much as I care about my own blood kids! They are our next generation. If they don't make it, we won't make it." This mirrored the feelings and concerns that had made me give up my plan to become a general practitioner in my hometown of East Chicago, Indiana, and work in education and child psychiatry. Thus, the third generation of my family's story, the black family story, is about my work with *all our kids*.

In Part I of this book my mother speaks: her story, her hopes and her dreams. In Part II I speak for myself and my brothers and sisters, who responded to the extraordinary effort made by remarkable parents. This extraordinary effort, against great obstacles, is the reason so many black people speak with pride about "the black family," and so bitterly resent those who focus on its weaknesses and ignore its achievements. And in Part III, I speak of my work and the role that I feel both black and white people must play to make it possible for many more black children to succeed.

Maggie's
American Dream

PART I

MOM

The Oral History of
Maggie L. Comer
as told to
James P. Comer

The Good Father

I was born in Woodland, Mississippi, to Jim and Maude Nichols. I had two brothers, Leroy and Frank, and two sisters, Seretha and Susie. I'm not able to tell you too much of what Woodland, Mississippi, was like. Being a child of five years old when my mother left Mississippi, I can't remember too much about it. But it was all rural area. They had little towns in the rural country like any other place, a couple of stores or so—that's all.

Most of the farming was sharecrop. It didn't leave the workers with anything to amount to. Woodland, as I can remember hearing from my mother talk about in later years, was very poor country. One year if they maybe were making a good crop, the boll weevils ate the crop. Then the next year they owed the man they worked for most of the crop, even though it was a good crop, because the boll weevils had ate the crop the year before.

My father was sharecropping. He had more education than the white man he was working for. My father did all his weighing of the cotton and taking care of his business because that white man could not read or write. There were about thirteen or fourteen boys in his family and some few of them got to go to school a bit. My father was one that did get to go to school. In fact, my father was the leader of their family of the thirteen or fourteen boys. He was the leader in a sense on the farm, but the white fellow

3

got the money. He did so well and this white man thought so much of him, he thought, "Well, our crops were so good this year, next year I'll start buying my own land and see what I can make." When he went to buy his own land from this white fellow he was sharecropping with, though, the man wouldn't sell it to him because he wanted him to stay on.

That was the year before he was struck by lightning.

I remember very little about my dad, but I remember that the children all gathered around him at all times. He thought so much of his little children. He took more care of us children than my mother did. He was an older man and he was very fond of little children. My mother said I was his favorite because they had two boys first, and then a girl—that was me. That's why I was the favorite. He always called me "Doll." I can remember my hanging onto him where he went. We children would hang onto him instead of my mother.

Pa's Dead

One day the small children was at home, and my father and stepbrother was in the field with my mother and stepsister. They saw clouds coming up. My mother's baby, Susie, was only six months old and was at home with me and Seretha. So when he saw the clouds coming up, he said to her, "You had better go home, it's going to rain and we only have a short corner here to finish. Son and I will finish it. You two women go on home and look after the children. I don't want you to get wet."

So they started home, but the shower caught them before they got home. The houses were far apart so they stopped at the first house they got to. They started, as the country people did, roasting sweet potatoes and peanuts in the fire and just having a good time. Then this awful storm came, thundering and lightning.

When the storm was about over, they looked out at the gate and saw my stepbrother lying on the gate. They started laughing at him and said, "Why don't you come on in? We told you to come on, you'd get wet." He laid there for a while, so they sensed something was wrong with him and went to the gate to see what was wrong. He said, "Pa's dead." They couldn't believe him. He said it two or three times. He had been shocked by the lightning himself.

He told how a hard clap of thunder nailed them against

a sycamore tree. He had looked over at my father and my father had looked at him, but he couldn't say anything. At that time the lightning came across and they both fell. There was a little creek by the side of the tree that my father was on. And when he fell, he fell in this little creek. My brother fell on the ground. My brother tried to pull him out of this creek; it was just a little creek of water. But he realized he was dead because he didn't speak or anything.

The way they got the news around in them days was to ring the bell. There was a big bell out in everybody's backyard, and if you heard that bell any hour besides twelve or six or times to go to and from work, that meant death; somebody had died in the neighborhood. After they went to the field and found that he was dead, they went to ringing this bell.

People started running from everywhere. They went down and pulled him up out of the water. The women brought quilts to take him to our house. About five, six men were carrying him on the quilt. It was in the summertime, grass was green. It was a long way and everywhere they stopped and laid him down, the grass burned up and the whole picture of his body was there. The lightning was still in the body. I don't know what that means, but I've heard my mother say many times that everywhere they put him down, that grass left the whole shape of the body. Some of the men went and clipped the grass away so that it wouldn't look like that for the family. Then he was buried.

This left a young widow with five children plus my father's two children, seven in all. (He'd had two daughters and a son, but one of the daughters was dead by that time.) My mother must have been in her late thirties when my father died. Well, as soon as he passed, his people took his kids, Son and Carrie, away from her because in them days they felt that this was the way to do it. Son and Carrie ran away a couple of times to come to be with her, to help her with us children, and if they had stayed with her, she probably would have been able to make it. But my father's parents wanted his kids. They were what you would call greedy. You see, when he died my mother halved everything he had with his two sets of children. The grandparents wanted them to come and live with them so they'd bring this half—a horse or two, a cow or two, and a hog or two. But after they got them, then they wasn't very nice to the kids.

We never seen the boy anymore at all because he died. The only thing I know about him was he was named Son, they called him Son and Duke. He lived quite a few years after the accident, but he was never a well person again. We don't know whether it was the shock of losing his dad like that, the lightning, or what.

Later on my stepsister, Carrie, got married to Charlie Watkins. She had one cow left that my mother had shared with her. She sold her cow to get his fare to come to East Chicago. When he got here, he started working in Inland Steel. When he made enough for her fare, he sent back and got her. Soon enough, they would have me too.

The Bad Father

My mother tried to work the land after Dad died. It didn't work because my brothers wasn't old enough to plow. That was the biggest thing about farming, you know. She got one of her sister's boys to live with us and help us do the crop, but there was only her and this boy. He was from a large family which was very close. In the evenings at his house they'd have such a good time together. So he didn't like being at our house with us little kids. My mother tried for a year, but it didn't work.

When that boy went back with his family, she didn't know what all to do. There was no help in them days. So she met this fellow that had been raised up there in Woodland. He had gone away to Memphis as a young man and got married. When he and his wife was divorced, he came back home, looking—like most men are looking today—for the woman that had the most. That was my mother, and he married her.

She had her cotton for the year and was set. She turned everything over to him, to let him sell everything else. He showed her the place where if she let him sell everything he'd take her to the city and give her a good living. Being a young widow she thought this was just fine. He got rid of everything she had, three horses, half dozen cows, and many turkeys and hogs.

He took us as far as Holly Springs, Mississippi. He told

8

her that he was going on to prepare a home for us in Memphis, but when he sent the fare back, he sent fare only for her. We were five children in a strange place. I was five or six years old. We had no food, no clothing, nothing. We just was living off neighbors in Holly Springs. Which meant that we were going to just die there or something if my mother left.

She didn't know what to do. So she just took all five of us and got on the train. When the train pulled off, the conductor came around to collect the tickets and she had one ticket for herself. The conductor—all of them was white then—took this one ticket and said, "Where's the ticket for these children?"

"I don't have any. They're not old enough."

"Oh, yeah, they're old enough. I can tell you the age of every one of these children." He had been at this business so long that he could practically look at you and tell. He told her, "I could stop this train right now and put you off."

We were way out from the station. He said again, "I could pull this train right now and put you and these children off. But I'm not going to do that. But don't you ever do a trick like this again."

So she went to tell him the story of how poor she was. Instead of pulling the cord and putting us off, he began to bring us fruit. At that time black people did not eat meals on the train. He felt so sorry for all these little children that he started bringing us fruit.

We came on then to Memphis. My stepfather was there waiting to greet her. He had no place for the rest of us, but he had to take us, she had brought us along. He found an old storefront—no beds, just junk. That's where we lived, sleeping on pallets.

Vagabonds

The early years in Memphis was very, very hard. My stepdad had a wife already in Memphis my mother didn't know about. So this means he had a wife on both sides of town. He wasn't divorced. He told her he was, but he wasn't. In those days nobody'd bother about poor colored people.

It was very hard in them days. Men couldn't make a living for one family, so you know how hard it was trying to make a living for two. He was a rustic furniture maker. He could have made good, but he was a poor manager. He left my mother several times, left us on neighbors.

We grew up there in Memphis. He had two children from his other marriage, a girl and a boy, Fred and Ethel. And there was my mother's five from her first marriage, me, Susie and Seretha, Buddy and Leroy. And later he and my mother had two children, Beatrice and Elizabeth. We all lived together—nine children in one house. The boys all slept in one bed and the girls all slept in one bed. We slept at one another's head and feet like sardines. We had old beds. The boys' bed was wire. There were quilts on them. We'd pull straw from the fields and put in the mattresses. And that would get flat and we'd put some more in.

He would go away and stay away months at a time, six months, a year at a time. My mother was such a friendly person. She would just move in a neighborhood and make herself acquainted, "Good evening, Miss Jones. How are you doing?" She'd make a conversation with people. We was friendly and we made friends everywhere.

My mother would say, "Go over there and tell Mrs. So-and-so I said send me a quarter." And she'd send it. "Tell Mrs. Smith I said to send me a few potatoes."

She would let the boys go downtown with a quarter. In them days there wasn't refrigerators like there is now. You had iceboxes and over the weekend you couldn't keep meat or chicken or what have you. So she'd have the boys tell the storekeeper to send whatever they could send us for a quarter. Soon the merchants, all white men, would catch on and would say, "Well, what are you doing later on tonight, boy?"

"Nothing."

"Well, hang around until I close the store, and all the things we can't keep over till Monday, we'll give to you." And sometimes they would give us enough food to last all week long. We were very smart children, if I have to say it, and were liked by most people, white and black. The boys were liked so much by everybody, and that's how we lived. Other than that, we could have starved and died.

But as soon as they would find out my stepdad was back with my mother, they wouldn't give us anything.

We moved from here to there and here to there, all more or less in the same area. People in them days moved every week or so. We lived on South Parkway most of the time, a couple of miles from downtown. The house was in a rural area just across the city limits—dirt roads, poor housing, poor people. We lived in many, many houses.

Most of the first houses we lived in was like barns. If they had any windows, they were open in the daytime. They let them out on a string. One didn't have any windows. You opened the doors, no screens. I can't remember any that didn't have floors that you couldn't jump across from one plank to the other. There were holes in the floors of some. My sister said that she used to sit in one house and count all the chickens under it. What happened back then was if you seen an empty house that was dilapidated, you just moved in. And when the person came to find out you moved in, then you talked with them. We must have lived in twelve or thirteen houses all together.

There were no lights, just lamps with coal oil and wicks in them. We were so poor we didn't own but one lamp. By night you had to have all you were going to do done. Because at night you had to go from one room to the other with this lamp.

We cooked on a coal or wood stove, mostly wood. You just pick up a board or plank or what have you around, and cook your meals. I think God in Heaven usually cooked the meals because I wonder now where we got enough wood to cook. At some of the places where we lived, there was simply no wood unless you pulled a board off the house to make a fire.

One of the houses that we lived in belonged to the man what used to be the mayor of the city, a Mr. Liddy. The mayor of the city in them days was somebody! There were quite a few acres around this house. This house must have had four or five rooms and that was big. So when the former mayor found out that somebody was living in the house, really his mother and father's house, he came out to see. He was so happy to find out that there was a family that had lots of children and wanted this place cleaned up. This was something he cherished, because it was where he grew up.

They had all kind of fruit trees and flowers, but weeds had overtaken the place. Because this family having all these children, he figured we'd be able to clean this place up, which we did. We made it just beautiful. My stepfather planted a garden. Mr. Liddy would come out and gather vegetables and fruit, and we'd help him. He thought the world of us children. My stepdad didn't pay any rent because Mr. Liddy thought so much of the way we cleaned the place up and took care of the property.

We were there about a year. As soon as my stepfather started making good there, he wanted to leave. He had my mother to move out of this Liddy house, and he left. She didn't know where to go, so she moved in a little settlement where a white fellow owned about twelve or more little houses, two-room houses. When this fellow came around to collect rent—he was a young white fellow—she didn't have any money. He said, "You want to work? My mother would like to have someone cook for her."

"Yes, I'd like to work."

"Well, we'll see about the rent, but you can go to work for my mother."

She worked for this white family for about a year. They would tell her every night—she worked until about seven or eight o'clock—to have one of her boys meet her. Whatever food was left over—they didn't keep food over then—she would take it home to her children. That's the way we ate. Also they owned a baker shop! Made cookies and donuts. And if they break a little piece they can't use, they just put them aside. He would never come to Mama to collect rent. Instead he'd always bring something like a charcoal bag full of cookies and bread. He'd always knock on the door and never ask for the rent.

As soon as my stepdad came back, he said, "Go and tell her I said come home and tell them that she won't be back." And she came on home, not knowing what to expect.

Now, what had happened was that he had moved us out of the Liddy house for this other family that he had. After about a year I guess something happened between him and this other lady, and he moved them out and moved us back in. And we lived in the Liddy house for another year.

Let me show you how smart he was. He could have made good. The telephone wasn't out in these rural places yet. So he and his brothers, Johnny and Bev, put up poles and strung up a telephone line from the city limits all the way out to Bunker Hill, where this Liddy place was, about a mile. He had built this little shack of a shop across the road from the house. And this phone was in a booth attached to the shop. All the folks in the area came and used the telephone when they needed it. There was two white grocers there in the area who used it almost every day to order their supplies. One was better off and he gave ten cents every time he used it. The other brought goods, mostly canned goods like salmon and peas.

The neighborhood folks usually paid a nickel when they used it. This was the new thing, the telephone. I remember once a friend of mine, Gracie Fetney Allen, was sick and her mother came there to call the doctor. She didn't know how to use the telephone and I was the one to show the people. I was just eight or nine years old, and she didn't want me to show her. So she went out there to use the phone. She was taking so long my mama had us peep through the window and see if she was okay. She was standing in there saying, "Hello, hello, Dr. So-and-so, Dr. So-and-so," and had not even picked up the receiver. She came back in and said the phone didn't work. So my mama sent me out there and I got the doctor right away.

But my stepdad threw away the money that he made from the things like that and we never got ahead. After one year there the second time, we moved again, leaving the shop, the telephone poles and everything. That's when we went on this houseboat down the Mississippi.

Down the Mississippi

He was a drifter. We left the Liddy place in Memphis and went to Arkansas, and then went to Dyersburg, Tennessee. I was about ten years old by then.

His brothers had built a little houseboat. He bought the engine so it made all three of them owners of the boat. And we all—three families—went down the Mississippi to Arkansas on that houseboat. They'd stop off when the food gave out—a little town, little country place, anywhere they could stop the boat. They'd go and see the fellow that owned the land. The owners always wanted somebody to pick cotton. My stepdad and his brothers and all would pick cotton until they got enough money to buy a little food and we'd move on farther.

There were twenty-one of us on a boat that was supposed to have three people. And there was three life jackets and twenty-one people, most were children. And whenever the police—they had police on the water just like on the land—come near, they'd say, "Say, where you niggers going?"

And Papa'd say, "Oh, we going up the river to pick cotton, white folks."

"You got any kids on there?"

"No suh, we don't have any kids." (They had us hide and we don't dare look out.)

15

And they'd say, "You got any life jackets?"

They'd say, "Yes suh, white folks" and hold up two or three. There was my stepdad, his two brothers, my mom, and two brothers' wives, and eight or nine of us children, and the brothers' children. Anyhow, there was twenty-one people on this little houseboat. My stepdad didn't care. He'd go on.

We were six weeks going from Memphis to Hickman Bend, Arkansas. The river was a mile wide and the levee was a mile from the river. People were farming all between the river and the levee. After a while the water began to rise and we had to bring the boat closer and closer to the levee. When the men came back, they had to jump from the land onto the boat. The boat rocked so I thought it was going to sink. One time it almost did.

This one night we didn't have any food and they kept on going. One would say, "Let's stop." And the other would say, "No." We finally got to a place where cotton was falling off, but the water was rising rapidly. They could only put the anchor down; there was no place to tie the boat up. The men jumped off the boat and climbed up the hill some way, going to look for food.

My mother was sitting on the boat and finally she said, "You know, I feel like this boat is sinking. Seems we're going round and round or something." And then my aunt said, "Maude, something is wrong!" And my mama said, "Yeah!"

They lifted the plank in the hull of the boat, and the hull was full of water. All the children grabbed buckets. Aunt Lillie could solder. She soldered that hull, but first we had to get all this water and pour it back in the river. We took rags and towels and dried up the hull, then she could put the solder on.

In the meantime a big boat trying to help us almost drowned us. They saw the light on top of our boat rocking from side to side, and they thought somebody was waving to come because they were in trouble. And so this big boat started toward us. It went *wssssssssh*, you know, those big waves. It was about to sink us. My brother run up on top of the boat and signaled them away. They went away and we didn't drown. But, oh, that was one of those times!

I didn't go off to pick cotton much. I was very little and also I was the cook. I had to cook for all twenty-one people. I would want to work in the fields because I was left at the boat picking greens, taking care of the fire, ordered to cook this for that one and that for another one. In those days you could get away with telling children to do anything if the parents didn't care. And those aunts wouldn't cook. They'd tell me to cook.

One time my brother was sent up on the boat deck to get something. We had a little junk on the deck. While he was up there, a chair fell off in the river. And my mama said, "Oh, my child is drowned."

My stepdad said, "Oh, what the hell, just one gone."

My mama went running to the door. He said, "Get back!" Bang, he slapped her. Meanwhile Buddy jumped on off to get the chair. When he got back, boy, did my stepdad beat him.

"You threw that out there," my stepdad said.

Now, why would Buddy want to throw a chair off the boat?

When we got to Hickman Bend, we lived between the houseboat and a little shack just beyond the levee. It was two rooms, cold and dark. We slept on pallets. There was a wood stove with two eyes. I cooked on that. There was thirteen of us in one house, and the rest was in another.

The water was still rising. At night you could hear it hitting up against the levee.

Again, my stepdad and his two brothers was smart and made a little money. Cows and horses and things got trapped in that rising water. They used the boat and the little skiff they had to rescue the animals. They'd tie a noose around their heads and pull them along, sometimes holding the heads up out of the water. Or they'd put a calf in the skiff and the cow would follow along behind.

Finally, the water rose so high in Hickman Bend, we had to leave. We went to Dyersburg, Tennessee, and stayed a while. My stepdad made furniture for the whole time we was there, but it didn't work out. We went back to Memphis.

We lived in a house that a colored lady had, Mrs. Hargarover. We lived in two rooms on one side, and she lived in the other. She was raising three children for a white man. They were his children by another colored lady. The children's mother died, so this white father got this lady to raise them. She used to drive a surrey and collect old clothes from the wealthy white folks and sell them cheap to poor black folks. You see, this man had a white family over the bridge in Arkansas, and these black children were not to be known about.

We was dirt poor, but people was nice to us, they really was. Mr. and Mrs. Caudee was the wealthy white folks nearby—my stepdad was buying land from Mr. Caudee. They was German people. Mrs. Caudee had this big garden and we kids used to help her with it. I remember the corn and beans and peanuts. I remember this water coming out of the mouth of the statue of a woman. She took us in this fine house of hers and I knew I wanted something like that for me.

We knew some of the better-off black people too. There was a Mr. and Mrs. Claustin my mama met through Mrs. Hargarover. He could pass for white. My mama used to visit with her and take some of us children. They had this fine place about a mile down the road from us. She and my mama used to sit and talk in this big yard that they had.

He was a strange man, very quiet—never mixed with her friends, just said, "Howdy." He owned property downtown and black folks couldn't go into some of his buildings. A clothing store was in a building he owned. His wife once went in the store to buy a cap for one of her children. This woman offered her a little cheap cap. Of course, they bought the best of everything. She started to tell her that she owned the building the store was in, but then she didn't. You know, black folks who had money had to be kind of careful back then.

And too, nobody knew how he got that money. He didn't seem to do anything but keep up with his property. The talk was that Mrs. Claustin was digging in a field one day near a clump of trees and hit something hard. She got him and they dug up a trunk or something full of money. And that's how folks say he got his money.

You can imagine how much I wished I'd dig up some money. Even then I was determined that life would be better. There was an alley between the city limits and the suburb. The white people was on the city-limits side, and we were on the suburb side. Only a wire fence separated us. The whites had much, much land around them. We lived upstairs and there was a little porch. I'd come out every morning and I would look over on this side: the colored homes, little toilets sitting outside, wire fences broken down, a pretty house here or there. And then I'd look on the other side: the whites, especially Mr. Caudee. He owned a fine house, acres of land around it. And there was Mr. Claustin. I'd see their daughters and things coming out in the morning, getting in their cars with their little grips. Some were lawyers and some were schoolteachers and so forth. And I'd always look over there and say—but it was all in my mind because I couldn't say anything out loud—"Why can't we live like that? Papa makes enough money and we do all we can, we're smart. Why can't we have something like that?"

If you said anything like, "Look at that girl, she got a new car."

He'd say, "Oh hell, that ain't for niggers, that's for white folks."

But that didn't dampen my spirit at all. When he would say things like that, he didn't know I'd just be swearing under my breath to myself. I'd say, "You damn so-and-so, if you would just try!"

I felt like those things were for anybody. I felt like if they could make it, I could make it! That's what I said to myself. If I said anything to my mother, she'd say, "Oh well, you know" . . . nothin'!

A Trifling Kind of Fellow

He was just a fool. Acted like a child with the white folks. First, black folks couldn't own a car. Then later on they couldn't get a license. But finally everybody had to have a license and a license plate. My stepdad didn't want to pay the money, so he went out and found an old plate—a New York license plate. They warned him several times to get a plate. When the policeman saw him with this New York plate he said, "Nigger, you'd better buy a license plate, you know you ain't from no New York!"

He paid no attention.

That's the sort of fellow he was. He heard what he wanted to hear. He worked when he felt like it.

My stepdaddy made rustic furniture. At times he would go way out to the country to sell his chairs and vases.

My stepdad and my brothers made beautiful vases. They made a stool with three legs and then they'd make a pot on top of it. They were made of wood. They would have to go into the woods and get willow or birch. They'd wrap it around the legs to make a flow-like thing on three sides. It was quite a bit of work, but they were very pretty. And the white people that bought that stuff sometime wouldn't have any money, but they would trade him chickens or corn or vegetables for those furniture.

He could have made good, but he did not. He was a trifling kind of a fellow. He was offered a job one time to

21

work in a place called the Superior Feed Company. They asked him to work there as a night watchman. Every hour during the night you had to push a button that would ring downtown to show that you were on the job. I remember the fellow came over and stood over his bed and begged him to take the job. He said, "No, I don't work for anybody." My brothers had got to be pretty good-sized boys at that time. So the man said, "Well, let the boys do it, just so the bell is rung every hour, let the boys do it." He refused that. He was one that didn't want nothing and you couldn't make him.

My brothers did help my stepdad make these flower baskets, benches, and so forth when he was there and they learned how. They started making them once when he went away and stayed so long and there was no food or nothing in the house. So they said, "Ma, let us make some benches and go out and see if we can sell them."

"No, if you touch those tools, Hon will kill you. Don't dare touch them."

They said, "Well, Ma, if we make benches and sell them, we can pay him for his tools."

Finally she agreed. And almost before they stepped outside the house, they came running back with the money. And after that they did that every time he would go away, make enough money for us to survive. When my stepdad would go away, people would buy them and say, "Well, I don't need it, but for you kids, here's fifty cents." But then my stepdad would go himself after he come back and people said, "No, we don't want yours. Some little boys come by and we buy from them." This made him awfully angry because it was his business. He'd mistreat the boys after that. It made it awfully hard. If the boys worked they got into trouble. If they didn't work, we starved.

One Mean Man

They weren't the only ones he mistreated. He was so mean to my mother. Oh, did he beat her! For anything. Someone else made him angry, and he'd come and beat her.

She was a poor young widow woman with a lot of children and didn't know what to do. My stepfather was the first thing she met, and that's the way she felt life was and had to be. And she went on with it. Whatever he did and whatever he said, she accepted. It got so he'd say, "Hon, so and so." Now, he had just knocked her out, but still she'd say, "Whatever you say, Hon." She'd be so scared she'd say something that he didn't like or it didn't work out, and she'd get another beating. She might as well said what she wanted to say. She was going to get the beating anyway.

She tried to send us to school when we first arrived in Memphis, but she couldn't. We'd go a day or two, and then he'd take us out. School didn't mean anything to him. He said we learned devilment in school and he didn't want us to go. We all wanted to go to school. We had nothing to do and all of us just standing around holding our hands and somebody would say, "Papa, can we go to school today?" Everybody got a whipping and cursing and kicking for that. I've seen him knock my mother cold sometimes for asking to let us go to school.

23

He wasn't only mean to us, my mother and his stepchildren. He wasn't nice to his own children either. One time he was so ugly that we were going to kill him. He had whipped my mother so for nothing; it just got to us. She was the only somebody we had to go to for anything. We didn't go to him. His little son said, "Let's kill him. We can kill him."

Whenever he'd whip her he'd always leave the house. He'd beat her up something terrible that day and left the house. Fred said, "Let's kill him when he comes back."

We said, "Okay."

"You take the hammer and you take the hatchet and you take this and you take that."

There was an old, big door about twice as big as us. And we all hid behind the door. We decided that when he came in, somebody was going to knock him in the head with the hatchet. And all of us were going to jump on him with whatever we had. My mother was laying out on the bed. The house got so quiet she started calling, "Children, children." Nobody answered. After a while she got up and come to look for us. It's a wonder we didn't hit her accidentally. We were all standing behind the door with these tools we were going to use to kill him with. She said, "Oh, put those things up! Hon going to kill you all!"

"Not if we get him first."

However, she made us put them down.

Many times, if it wasn't that I was caring for my sister Susie, I would have been in somebody's jail. Susie was sickly when she was young, and there was nobody to care for her but me because he didn't allow my mother to do anything for her. I used to slip bread under the cover for her, or medicine when she was sick. One of the neighbors would get medicine for me and I would slip it to her.

Many times I had the opportunity to get rid of him and I thought about doing it. We'd be standing on a bridge and I'd be standing behind him: boy, I could . . . ! I didn't care what they would do to me, but I would think about what would become of Susie.

I've known some mean, mean men and mean women, but I don't know of anybody ever being as mean as my stepdad. He just went out of his way to mistreat us. Whenever he was going to leave home all the children would go "scamping" to find his hat because we were so glad to get rid of him. He never played with us. He didn't even allow my mother to take up any time with us. My mother, being an orphan herself, felt the need of being with us. But she was afraid even to talk with her children when he was around.

When he was gone, we would joke and run and play. One of the games we played was ragball, throwing the ball over the house, saying, "Annie Over." I don't know how many people remember that. Back when we couldn't buy a ball, we would wrap string around a rag and make a ball out of it. We'd throw it over the house and then we'd throw it back. There was no such thing as going out for recreation in those days. We played tag, hitting each other and run, Hide-and-go-seek.

But he wouldn't let us play when he was around. There was some games that he didn't like. One of them went like this: "How many miles to Bethlehem?"

And the other side would say, "Three score and ten."

"May I get there by candlelight?"

"Not without your bow and bend." And then you'd do a little twist. I still can't figure out what was wrong with the words, but he didn't allow it. And there wasn't nothing really wrong with the little twist. But something was wrong with anything that was a joy to us children.

We had no toys. Well, almost none. One year when he was away, my mother worked out as a cook. And I can remember sneaking and looking in the trunk that she had. She had bought a doll. It was for me, and it was the only doll I ever owned as a child.

He was just a mean, violent man. He didn't drink and

he didn't smoke. But he was one mean man. There wasn't much ugly that he didn't do.

He said terrible things, terrible. "There wasn't nothing to religion! There was no God." He hated preachers. He couldn't stand the minister to come around. One minister came to the house to tell him about coming to church. He told the minister there was no such thing as God.

Oh, he was the devil himself. When he was going to spend money for food, he wouldn't do it on Saturday like everybody else. He would wait until Sunday about twelve o'clock, when everybody else was gone to church or coming from church, and he'd send us down to the store. He'd say, "Everybody eat up every damn thing I can make. Go down there and get this or that or the other."

Everything at the store is picked over. And sometimes we'd be coming down the street with a live chicken (they didn't kill the chicken in them days) and the other little girls all dressed up, coming from church or sitting out on the swings. And we had an old chicken going, "Cluck, cluck, cluck." It was embarrassing!

We didn't even go to church until the year before I left home. There was a missionary lady that lived with her sister. A revival was going on and she would go around the neighborhood and ask the folks to let their children go to church. I remember her coming by arguing with him, oh, several times, "Let me take these children to church." One reason why he didn't want us to go to church was that he didn't want to buy clothes. That's the same reason he didn't want us to go to school. He didn't want to buy books and so forth. After Carrie and my brother Leroy started sending us clothes from up North, though, she finally got him to let us go to church.

"Friends" Before Family

His family would be hungry at home, but he would give things to other people to make friends. And people would say, "Mr. So-and-so is a nice man. He gave me this." See, after a while he stopped making furniture at all. Now the boys made the furniture and gave the money to him. He would start home and before he got there, he'd give Sister So-and-so a dozen eggs, he'd give Sister So-and-so a chicken, and then he'd get home and we'd ask him, "Poppa, how many chickens can we cook?" He'd go to swearing, "You eat up everything."

Oh, he grinned and carried on with the neighbors all the time. He thought he was making friends. But years after we were grown and would come home, these same people would mention how bad he treated us—and how little they thought of him.

There were two of them that visited, Armour, a great, big old man, I've forgotten the other one. When they came, my stepdad would tell me, "Cook a chicken." And he'd say to his friends, "Come on and have some dinner."

And they'd say, "No, I'm going home. My old lady will have some dinner."

"No, it don't taste like mine, come on." Oh, he was so insistent!

Finally they would accept. I have seen them sit down and eat and drink and when they got up from the table there'd be nothing left but bones. And they would sit there arguing the Bible or something for hours. And we would wait and wait for them to leave. They ate all the food, and didn't even look around or ask if there was enough for the children!

Sometimes when there was nothing left my mother would say, "Go tell Miss Sarah I said send me a quarter."

You see, there was a colored lady named Sarah who lived across the street from us. They had a nice house. She did housework for white people, though she was pretty well-to-do, according to my father and mother. I think their father had money. He built this house for his two daughters. Miss Sarah had one section, and the other sister had the other. Miss Sarah worked practically every day. She was ambitious, walked dignified, looked nice. I admired her. And she could see up the steps to our house so she could see people go up and down.

On holidays or Sundays, she'd see my stepdad's friends go up. Later on she'd call and say, "I saw Armour go up there. I know he ate up all the food. Bring a bucket and come on over and get some food."

Miss Sarah would fill up a bucket with food, and tell us to stop over there and tell Lucille, her sister, to put some food in it. She and her sister didn't like each other. But she'd say, "Tell Lucille I said to put some food in this bucket!" And she did.

What he gave away to our neighbors, our neighbors ended up giving behind his back to us.

Once he took us way out somewhere to pick blackberries. He told us we'd better come back with full pails or we'd get a beating. He and my mom sat around the truck and picked a few berries but not many. Now, his son, Fred, couldn't see well, so he didn't pick many berries. The rest of us had full pails when we got back. He beat that boy something awful, all down in the dirt and so on.

He sent us all back to pick another pail of berries. Each one of us put berries in our own pail and some in Fred's pail. Fred had more than any of us that time. My stepdad started, "Now, see there, I knew that boy could pick berries like anybody else." That shows you how big a fool he was.

When we drove back home folks was sitting out. He stopped the truck and gave berries to this one and that one all along the road. And there we was sitting scratched and dirty, his son had been beaten, and he was giving away the berries.

There was so many times there wasn't any food. There was so many times there wasn't anything but salt on the table. I've seen my mama go by the table hungry and lick a little salt.

Back then I did the cooking. The first meal I cooked, I was seven years old. I made biscuits. I can remember very well it was biscuits. My mother was sick at the time. She couldn't walk and he was gone. But there was some flour there. She told my brother how to put me on a box to a cabinet. I could see her from her bed, and she told me how many cups of flour and so forth. And believe it or not, I got those biscuits all done. It was like salmon croquette or something like that to me. I was so proud. By the time I got this meal all done, he walked in. We hadn't seen him in over six months, I bet. He walked in and ate up most of that meal.

Now, when my momma and stepdad ate, we never could eat with them. He never allowed the children to come to the table with adults. We had to wait and if there was anything left, we got it. He'd need a fan in the summertime. We had to stand and fan him while he ate. And in one house we were in he made a fan on a pulley string. He had us hid, you know. He had built a paste-board fan and he put a pulley string on it. We had to stand behind him out of sight and pull the string. This would cool him as well as keep the flies away.

My mother would sit down and eat a little, but she'd feel so bad because the children couldn't eat. So many times she would pinch so that the children could have something left. My mother never tried to stand up to him.

It's no wonder that the first time Leroy came home after he ran away, as soon as he said, "Hi," to everybody, he said to my mom, "I want to go and buy some food." And of course, by then my stepdad had a little pickup truck. Leroy must have had about fifty dollars, and in those days fifty dollars would fill a truck. He brought back a barrel of flour, barrel of sugar and meat, and all kinds of stuff.

When Leroy came back, I cooked this meal. Several people came to dinner: the man next door, Mr. Perkins, and others. The man from next door said, "Now, you should let the children, at least let Leroy eat with you all, since he's grown now." Leroy had bought the food.

My stepdad said, "Yes, yes, that's what I'm gonna do. Alright, Leroy, come on and let's eat."

Leroy said, "No, that's alright, you all go ahead and eat. I'm gonna wait for the children." And this just killed my stepdad.

He said, "You better come on, they'll eat up everything."

Leroy said, "That's alright, I'll get some more. But I'll wait and eat with the children."

Later, whenever anybody went back home the first thing we would do was to buy some groceries. This would help the younger children. It was quite a life.

Good-Bye Tennessee

Leroy ran away first. He was working for a drugstore delivering small medicines to the white people in town on a bicycle. But he was so raggedy that he was almost bare. So one day when the man paid him he said, "You will have to buy some pants with a portion of this. I can't have you going up to people's door with pants like that."

So my brother bought the pants and came home and brought my stepdad the rest of the money. He told him, "Mr. Frankel told me that I had to buy some pants, so I bought the pants." And he got a whipping for buying pants out of the money he was paid. He was sixteen years old, and my stepdad was whipping him with long willow switches. So that day he ran away.

We had all been planning to run away. For a year each one of us had been saving a nickel or a dime from our errands. We would drop it in an old tin can that we hid. The plan was that Leroy would run away and save money and help us all leave. So finally after he had hit Leroy and he didn't come back, my stepdad kept asking, "Where's Leroy?" We all just looked at each other, grinning when he wasn't looking. Finally that evening we heard the whistle of the boat, the *Charles Organ*, at six o'clock. We knew Leroy was gone.

A very similar thing happened with Buddy. I remember he made a deal with a fellow: He was to go over to Arkansas, right across the bridge from Memphis, to help this fellow's brother gather a crop. My stepdad always kept a little pickup truck but only with one or two tires on it; the rest was on rims. My stepdad took this truck down piece by piece and couldn't get it to run, so he left it laying in the yard in pieces. So my brother put the car back together and got it to run. And he was able to take that job.

Some men working in a school needed to move some chairs. So they asked my brother about using the truck. He used the truck and helped them move the chairs. But he was so raggedy that they told him, "Now you take some of this money and buy some clothes." Again my stepdad whipped him 'cause he took a small part of the money to buy clothes like the man told him. Buddy ran away too. That shows you just what kind of person my stepdad was, foolish as well as evil. One had already run away and he did the same thing to the other.

Buddy was going to kill my stepdad. He hid under the bed waiting for him with a gun. But we got him out of there. Because there might be trouble, Leroy got him the money to go up North.

After Buddy left, I wrote Leroy that I was really ready to leave there. He wrote back and told me that my half sister, Carrie, was coming down that summer and that he'd send my fare by her. I was sixteen on August first, and I left August first. If you ran away before you were sixteen they could force you back home. So I waited until I was sixteen.

He didn't want me to go. He put up this story that I couldn't leave because this was going to be a banner year for the family, that they would need me there because my mother had to follow him around on the truck. He couldn't read and write and she could. And he was wondering who was going to do the cooking.

You could imagine what I was saying under my breath. I put up a false front. When he said I couldn't go until December, I said, "Oh no, I don't want to go there in the wintertime. I hear that people freeze. I would rather go now in August and come back before December." He believed that, but I didn't mean it at all. When the train pulled out of the station, I said, "Good-bye, Tennessee."

He finally asked my mother when I was coming back. My mother was scared, but she said that I wasn't coming back. All hell broke loose at that time.

It was seven years before I went back to see my mother and my sister. My stepdad was there in the house, but I didn't go back to visit with him.

Things had changed. By this time only his and my mother's children were left at home. He'd say, "Liza, get me a glass of water." She didn't move. I said, "Liza, didn't you hear your dad ask for some water?" I was kind of nervous thinking she was going to get a beating. She said, "I'm not thirsty, let him get some water himself if he wants it." Now, that was different. I don't know what brought about that kind of change, whether it was my mother finally standing up to him and going off to the church, his getting religion, or what it was, but that was different!

East Chicago

In August 1920, I came into Chicago on a train. Me and Carrie got off the train in Chicago and we took the streetcar into East Chicago, which was about thirty miles away. I didn't stop to think too much about Chicago or East Chicago. All I wanted was freedom. I thought, "I can make it anywhere!"

East Chicago was just a few houses, and most of it was steel mill and smoke. There wasn't any finery or anything of the kind, but that wasn't what I was looking for. I was looking for a better life for myself. To hear people talk about Chicago, as I had heard my sister talk when I was still in Memphis, you'd think that money was dropping off of trees. They would say that you just didn't have to want for anything; you could have whatever you want. While still down South, I thought to myself, I'll wait and see what it's like. And, sure enough, East Chicago wasn't what I had been told. It was quite a letdown. You know when people in the South long years ago said Chicago or East Chicago, Indiana, they claimed: this is heaven. But I never did believe it.

East Chicago was quite different from Memphis. When I first came to East Chicago most of the people were two races, Polish and blacks—very few Spanish, if any. And there weren't that many black folks. In Memphis the well-off people was on one side of the track and the poor were on the other. In East Chicago you didn't have that gap. We were most on the same level; everybody worked at the steel mill practically. There was only a doctor or so and a dentist. Also there was a vast difference in size, East Chicago being a town and Memphis a huge city.

My brothers and brother-in-law worked at Inland Steel at the time. My brother-in-law, Charlie Watkins, and my brother Leroy worked all of their lives at Inland. Leroy was hired at Inland when he was sixteen years old, and he retired when he was sixty-five. So he worked fifty years at Inland.

Your uncle Buddy worked there too. But he didn't work there for long. He left and went to St. Louis and Milwaukee. He was the kind to change around a bit when he was young. Finally he came back to East Chicago and lived here most of his life too.

When I first came into East Chicago there wasn't much segregation. As I said, there were only two nationalities of people, Polish and blacks. We didn't speak their language and they didn't speak ours. But you could live on any street in East Chicago, even Grand Boulevard—my best friends lived on Grand Boulevard. Fifteen years later, it had become one of the finest streets in town—and white only.

Sis Carrie's

I lived with my half sister, Carrie, and her husband, Charlie Watkins. My two brothers were also living with her at that time. My brothers and I had planned for me to go to school because my stepfather would not let us go in Memphis. They wanted somebody in the family to get an education.

We had learned some in Memphis. We hid some books around that different people would give us. At night when he was away we'd study those books, but we had to run and hide them when we heard him coming. Of all the days put together I hadn't had six months of school in Memphis. I would be two or three days in school when it started in September. Then we wouldn't go anymore until a few days just before Christmas, and a few more just before school was out in the summer. And that's what few days I got in schooling. We was never bought a set of books.

So I wanted to go to school in East Chicago, but I was a little bit too old at the time, at sixteen. I had to be put in the class with eight-year-old children. But I learned a lot going to school in East Chicago a little while. The teacher and children was nice to me. They got interested in me when they see I was a great big girl and I didn't know how to read and write. I got quite a bit of help from them. Soon I was able to read and write my name and count to one

36

hundred and so forth. However, I had to do too much work at home. I would have to rush home and cook for the whole family—for her husband, my two brothers, her, and a couple of roomers she had. Then I had to wash clothes until twelve or one o'clock at night. I could not do all that and go to school. I don't feel anything bitter toward Sis Carrie. She felt like it didn't make sense for a great big girl like me to be in beginning school.

Living at Sis Carrie's was quite a step up for me. Brother Charlie made good money at the time. They were buying their own home, a six-room house in a nice neighborhood. They were church people, and we hadn't been allowed to go to church back in Tennessee. They had plenty of food, which we did not have back in Memphis. I did get to wear some of her hand-me-downs, which was quite a privilege at the time. But still I had a mind that this wasn't it yet. I was very independent and I wanted to be on my own.

There was not much recreation at Sis Carrie's. Brother Charlie was a deacon of the church and very strict. Few of my brothers' friends ever came to the house. I don't know how far he would have gone with that kind of thing, but my brothers knew it wasn't their house. They hadn't known him before and they stayed at what they thought was in the distance of what he allowed. Brother Charlie brought friends from church every now and then for dinner or just to sit. The recreation was visiting. People would just come and sit and talk all afternoon, until wee hours of the morning. Talk about back home. It really wasn't very in-teresting to me. I didn't want to hear about back home.

Of course, I was kind of cautious too. I wasn't too sociable. My brothers suggested that I go live with a cousin and go to school when it didn't work out with Sis Carrie. (My father's brother's daughter was the only cousin I really knew because my mother left Mississippi when I was five or six years old. When she left to go to Memphis, the majority of the people left Mississippi to go to New York. So consequently we didn't get to know our cousins except this one.) When we knocked on the door somebody said, "Come on in!" When I walked in there were a bunch of men playing cards and drinking. My brother introduced me to them and it started, "Oh, Lee, is that your sister? Oh, oh, oh man!"

I never did care for a lot of foolishness: playing cards, sitting around, loafing, as I would call it. That kind of sitting around, up to nothing, bothered me then and it still bothers me today. I thought even back then that black folks had lost enough time because of slavery. They should be thinking of things of interest to them or things that was going to help them get ahead instead of saying, "Oh man, that piece of steel fell in the mill the other night," or "Man, I climbed that tree" or this or that. You know, just wolfing.

So I knew from the start that I wasn't going to stay there. Both brothers had tried hard to make it possible for me to go to school, but I wouldn't go through all that. This was when I really gave up on the idea of going to school.

Catch as Catch Can

After I had to leave school, I went out and knocked on door after door asking, "Would you like to have a girl to work?" Most of the work in the two years before I was married was catch as catch can.

At first I held jobs for two or three weeks at a time. People were poor back in them times. They weren't wealthy enough to hire people for more than a day a week or a couple weeks at a time. Most of the people did their own work.

Being a girl from the South, my attitude was different to the kids in East Chicago. They wouldn't go out looking for work like that. My attitude was how I got my first real job, in a candy store.

It was a Sunday and this bunch of girls got together and went from Sunday School to this store where the kids would always go. That was my first time of being there. The kids here in East Chicago was used to doing different than we was back in Tennessee. When they rushed in, everybody was saying, "I want, I want, gimme this, gimme that." And I stood back because I wasn't used to that sort of thing. Some would pick up something that didn't belong to them. The lady that owned the store, she was watching me very closely. And I'm standing back because I don't do that. I wait until everybody's through and ask for

39

what I wanted. Just before the kids all left, she said, "You, girl, I want to see you a minute."

I hadn't did anything, but I wondered, "Now, did she think I had picked up something?" I stood aside. She let all the other children go, and then she asked my age and where I lived and so forth. And she said, "Would you like to work?"

"Oh sure I would!"

"Well, I would like to have you work for me. If you come tomorrow morning I'll talk with you."

The work was awfully hard. She put as much work on me as you ought to put on three people. But I was happy to have it at that. I did housekeeping and washing; as a sixteen-year-old girl I was washing for a family of five. You ironed all day one day and washed all day the next. I also helped her make sandwiches to sell at a school. And I did all the scrubbing down on my hands and knees. But not cooking, 'cause she was Jewish and I wasn't able to cook their way. I didn't have time anyway. If there was ever any minutes left after I finished washing and ironing before the day was gone, I had to work in the store.

I'd sell ice cream. Kids come in for an ice cream cone or candy, whatever, I was allowed to do that. She had so much confidence in me. Although I worked awfully hard, she was really nice to me. She paid $10 a week, which was surprising at that time because that was more than some of the women were making. But I worked from seven to seven, sometimes more, and seven days a week. I got off at noon on Sunday.

She was the first person that taught me about savings. She had two daughters, Sarah and Pearl. The older daughter was home and the other went to school. Pearl and I wore the same size dresses and shoes, so she gave me their clothes. She asked me what was I doing with my money since I didn't have to buy clothes, and I told her I was giving it to my brother-in-law to keep for me. She said, "No, you don't need to do that. Pearl goes to the bank every Monday morning. If you want me to keep your money until Monday, I will give it to you and you can go with Pearl. She will help you start your own bank account." And that's what I did. But that wasn't very well welcomed back at home.

I worked at this job for quite a while, until I was forced off. Somebody told the truant officer that I was working and not in school. He came and talked to the lady that I was working for and told her what would happen to her if she didn't let me go so that I could go to school. I was going on seventeen; I didn't have to go back. But I was young and I didn't know. And the lady probably didn't want any trouble. I don't know the true situation, but I had to stop working there.

And of course I was very honest. When I started working for a lawyer's wife, Mrs. Brissey, there was a fifty-cent piece and a dollar laying in different places in the house. She had put that there on purpose. I realized as soon as I seen them what it was for. I would dust and put them right back where they was. So then after a while she would trust me with anything.

But I did have a friend to come in and move some change. She had said that I could have company, and I brought this girl to stay with me while I worked. She took the money and some fruit and left. When I looked and the money was gone, I was so scared. I said, "Now this child has left with that money and this lady has gone to Chicago." What was I going to do?

I didn't have that kind of change to put back. So as soon as the lady came in, I explained to her. "This week when you go to pay me, you hold money back because I am responsible for bringing that little girl here." And even though I asked her to take the money out of my salary, she didn't do it. She said she knew as long as I had been there, money hadn't been moved.

A big part of my education came while I was working for this lady. In the wintertime I didn't go home until after dinner, but during dinner I would just sit around. She finally asked me if I wanted some books. So she dug out her old books that she had had in school and let me have them to study. At the same time, there was a poor white girl that would come over for the leftover doughnuts and so forth. I would save for her. So we decided to exchange. She would give me a lesson every day and I would save her food. She was much younger than I was, but we had a good time. She was a lovely little girl. As a joke, if I didn't have my lessons when she would come, she would tap me on the hand with a pencil. That is where I really learned to read and write, what little bit I did.

Life Was Mostly Church

When I came to town in 1920, Zion Church was a storefront on Elm Street. In 1921 it started to build a basement, just a basement, where it is now on Drummond Street, and of course they stayed in the basement for years. When they moved to Drummond Street, we all walked down the street on Sunday carrying a Bible or chair from the old church. It took some time for them to finish it—it wasn't too many of our people in East Chicago at that time and many of them were not church people. Today it's one of the largest churches in East Chicago and one of the most outstanding.

At that time blacks didn't have any stores in East Chicago. They tried to have a coop store at the church for a time, but it didn't work out because all the members— there were like twenty men—wanted his wife and his daughter to work in the store and there was confusion. They had to dissolve it. It wasn't exactly a store from Zion Church, but it sprung out of the Zion Church members.

Life was mostly church. You went to church on Sunday from morning until eleven o'clock Sunday night. You'd go for dinner and back to church to night service. And then during the week you had about three nights that you went to choir rehearsal and prayer service. Your recreation was really church and church socials.

I didn't have a lot of close friends because girls were so

43

. . . well, there wasn't many my type of girls. But the girls I knew were from around the church. Lucille Tonsel was one, and Irene Lawhorn was another, and Hazel Peterman— that was her married name, I can't think of her other name— and Roberta Floyd. That was the preacher's daughter.

To go around with the preacher's daughter was something. She was the leader of the group of girls, the one that we all looked up to. Now, you had to be a very nice girl to be able to go in her group. I didn't get to spend a lot of time with them because I usually had to work on Sunday when I worked steady. But even then I was sometimes off at twelve and I could go to three o'clock service, or I was off at five and I could go to seven o'clock service.

That's how I met your dad, at church with this group of girls. He was looking for the nice kind of girl that was in this preacher's daughter's group.

Mr. Comer

Hugh Comer was as near perfect a man as there can be. He didn't smoke. He didn't drink. He didn't care for the wild life. If he told you he was going to do something, you could bank on it . . . and honest as the day is long. They don't make men like that anymore—except his sons, of course.

He came to town before me, in 1916. I first knew him when he was an usher in our church. He was such a nice gentleman they made him one of the trustees of the church. On from that he was made the highest position, next to the minister, deacon of the church.

When I first came to East Chicago I was sixteen years old. At sixteen in them days, you dressed like a girl, and he didn't pay much attention to me. He was dating another girl that was older.

In 1920 he went back South for a few months. In the meantime I changed my way of wearing clothes and dressed more like a young lady. When he came back he didn't recognize me. He asked the preacher's daughter, "Say, who is that girl?" He had been looking at me. "That's Charlie Watkins' sister-in-law," she said, "you remember."

That next Sunday, he came on down to our house after church. We lived just a block away. Somebody would always come with my brother-in-law every Sunday evening, just sit awhile until the next service. I said, "Have

45

a seat, my brother-in-law will be out in a few minutes."
He said, "I didn't come to see him. I came to see you."
And that's how it started.

I thought, "Come to see me? What's he talking about?"
He was such an outstanding young man, I didn't think I
was equal to such a person. All of the people around and
in the church felt he was a nice guy. He went to church
and he worked. He wasn't a playboy or mess around:
foolishness, as I would call it. He was very serious.

He was stern about the things that he believed in: religion and education and just plain being somebody. That
was his all-around person. He believed you could live the
better way of life. He always felt that black people could
get the better way of life just like everybody else, though it
didn't seem so.

Like I say, he was a very serious type of person. Even
his first talk—we were almost engaged the first time we
talked. At that point I was afraid of men. I had no really,
you know, backing. I had heard how so many men had
come into town and pretended they never had been married and disappointed girls. When the girl knew anything,
this man's wife and children would come. But Hugh Comer
was so frank about his life and this turned me from thinking that all men were alike.

I had not really dated before, except going out at the
church. That's as far as you could go—with my sister and
her husband walking behind you and the boy. And you
better not get behind them! Fellows could come to the
house, but it had to be fellows my brother-in-law knew.
He had younger brothers and other friends who would
come to the house. But we was just kids playing the
record player—girls and boys.

Sometimes the church socials were held at our house
(the social was at different homes because what little dancing the kids could do, the two-step and so on, they didn't
allow at the church then). They always liked to have it at a
home where there was a piano. As a rule, out of the group

somebody could play the piano. Sis Carrie and Charlie had one, so many of the socials were at our house. I remember your dad coming to our house to a social with this older girl when I was just counted as a little girl. It was awfully heartbreaking for her later on when she found out we were marrying. He was quite a catch. Like I said, he was one of the most outstanding young men around the church.

I wasn't paying him any attention until he opened up with his life. I was almost afraid of men at that time. But when he opened up with his life it kind of made me think, "Well, this fellow is for real and . . . honest." Right away he wanted to get married. He wanted to settle down, and I was the type of girl that he thought he'd settle down with.

He was very honest. He told me he'd been married and he had a daughter, Louise. He told me he and his wife was divorced. At first I said, "No, no, you've been married."

"But me and my wife have divorced and my wife is also married again. She is in Hartford, Connecticut."

He seemed honest but I didn't take that. I was always looking out for me. I said, "Oh, well, you and your wife might go back together someday, and I don't want to go between any man and his wife."

Again he told me that she was remarried. I still didn't take that from him. He had to write his mother-in-law and his mother and have them verify what he had told me. His mother-in-law wrote a very nice letter saying that she thought he was a nice fellow and she thought her daughter wasn't ready to settle down. His mother also wrote a nice letter. And after they wrote back I felt like he was okay. But I didn't give no date at all until I read those letters and he brought the proof of his divorce from this lady, which I have today.

I wasn't taking any chances. I remember not more than two or three times of going out and getting back after dark with him. That would be from some church affair that we'd gone to and it held over late. I'd be so scared that he'd have to tell me, "Don't worry, I'm not going to hurt you." He was a very nice man. He said what he meant in the first place, and meant what he said.

Brother Charlie and Sis Carrie liked him. She knew right away when we started dating, being the fellow that he was, that she was going to lose me. Now, she didn't dislike him at all, but it was a fact that she didn't want to lose her helper. So she tried to discourage us—me, at least. She called him "old pa" because he was twelve years older than I was. She'd see him coming down the street and she'd start, "Here he comes. Where is he going? What do he want?" It was quite funny because I knew what she was doing. She was trying to put me against him—putting him down. One time I said to her, "Oh, Sis Carrie, don't say all that, you'll make me dislike him." But I didn't really mean that. I could tell what she was after.

Me and Mr. Comer got along right from the start because we had the same thing in mind—getting ahead, getting our own home. We expected a family. He wanted children and he wanted them educated. This was the kind of thing he preached until he died.

What he said about education, and everything else too, was what I had fought for. As a child, all around me kids went to school and were educated and came out with a degree and went into good jobs. This was the thing I wanted my children to have. This was the right man.

Mr. Comer's family was a little better off then mine. Of course, that didn't take much. He was born in Comer, Alabama. I didn't really get to know his mother—Dixie was her name. I corresponded by mail, but I met her only once. She and two of her daughters spent three weeks with us and she was a lovely person. I had planned to spend the next vacation with her, but she passed away. I never met his father, Morgan. He had passed before we was married. He was a minister.

I spent about three weeks at his home down South after his mother passed. When we got there they had the wagons and the buggies waiting to take us out to the home.

There wasn't running water or sidewalks. The lights were the lamps that you carried in your hand, you know, coal oil. But it was very nice. Your dad had bought a home there on about thirty acres of land. He had built this house for his mother and that's where we stayed. It was pretty. They had pecan trees and different fruit trees. It was very nice but very country.

There was a post office, a church, a courthouse—those few buildings, a couple of streets, and that was it. The train went through the center of town and the station was right there. And whenever the train stopped people from out in the rurals would come in just to see the people that got off the train.

There were two sets of Comers—the white Comers and the black Comers. They both were large families. The town was started by the white Comers, of course. They were very nice to the black Comers. There was a tie because the black Comers had been slaves to the white Comers and some of them still worked for them. Some did very well there. Your dad's two sisters, Madie and Rebecca, worked for Governor Comer—yes, he was the governor of Alabama.

The white Comers had sold off much of their land, and the black Comers bought some of it. The black Comers all lived together in the same area—the Comer Quarters, as they called it. Everybody was a member of the family. They all gathered in one yard and talked; they all went to the same church. Comer, Alabama, was just a family of people.

Your dad liked to talk about his childhood. His parents were very strict, very religious, and believed in education. All of the older ones went to school. Your dad went to what they called college in those days—it was an academy—for eight years. They weren't able to carry you as high in the black schools then as they are today. He was one of the most outstanding students they ever had. I remember some of the fellows from the South teasing him about being such a good student and making it hard on them. He was also an outstanding baseball player. He was a real leader, they told me. He was an independent kind of person and didn't believe everything he was told. He told me a funny story about this once.

In those days people believed in "haints." I guess some do today. Your dad was going along a road that people said was haunted and he heard this noise. When he walked, the noise walked. When he stopped, the noise stopped. At first he thought it was this "haint" and he was getting afraid. Most people would have run off and believed it was the "haint." But finally Hugh looked into the bush off the road and there was a little dog. He said he never believed in "haints" after that.

He came North the last time because the boll weevils ate up the cotton that year. He and his two sisters, Madie and Rebecca, was all in school. That crop was what they were depending on that fall. The crop failed and all of them was going to have to come out of school if he stayed on there. So he left and came here to help those two sisters. They went on to school for another year.

Also, his father was buying this land. When he lost the crop he couldn't pay on the land so it was going to go back to the white Comers. When your dad came here he made some money and take over the payments. But he didn't take it over in his name; he just took up the notes in his dad's name and finished paying for it. It was never his. After his father died it went to everybody. He only had a child's part. But he paid for the land.

He was the first one to leave out of that neighborhood going away to the place they call Chicago. It was really East Chicago, Indiana. He left his people crying. Nobody from there had ever been to Chicago.

He stayed at this place where this fellow had a tent, where they just sleep men mostly. There was no black women, or not any up to any good. They slept in tents until they made a few paydays and then they rented rooms or a house. He rented a house and kept a few renters, and then he sent back for a couple of his relatives.

He first planned to work and go back, like so many others. So many of the people that came here back in those days didn't come here to stay. They didn't like it here. They didn't like the weather. It was so different to their way of life at home. It was hard for people raised in the South to adjust to the city type of life. This was almost like being in jail for them, living in apartment houses with a postage-stamp lawn. They was used to spread-out fields and crops, fishing ponds. They didn't come here to stay. You couldn't talk them into that; they thought you were crazy.

I was talking to a lady from the South when your dad and I build our first house. She seen the house going up, and she had heard that we were building it. I met her in the street one day and she stopped me and said, "Girl, are you all crazy? His mother and your mother is in the South and you all building a house here. Are you losing your mind?"

That's how people felt about this place at the time. That's one of the reasons our people haven't accomplished any more than they have. We paid a part of it out to the railroad traveling back South. The fellows would work three months and run home, work three months and run home. And then they brought their wives and the wife had to go back home to see Mama. And if they got expecting a baby they had to go back home. They couldn't stay here because they was away from Mama or away from the South.

Not us. We was there to stay.

And We Was Married

Mr. Comer had decided to stay up North even when we started courting. When he asked me if I would marry him and I said yes, he asked me who he should ask. Should he write and ask my mother, or ask my sister? So I said you write and ask my mother, but you can tell my sister. So when he told Sis Carrie that she said, very slowly, "Well, I don't mind you getting married, but I want you all to live with us because you see we have Buddy rooming here and I won't be able to take care of him alone. You all can have that other bedroom there."

My brother Buddy was her roomer, not mine. Right away Mr. Comer said, "No, I won't promise that. I plan to go into a house of my own."

He wrote my mother and she wrote him back. She said it was alright, but she wanted me to come home first. "No," Hugh said. "I'll send you home the next day after we're married if you want to go, but not before."

I didn't go.

Even so, the marriage didn't come off the way we wanted it. Just before I got married, Buddy took sick with pneumonia. He was as sick as I've ever seen a person. My husband-to-be sat up with us at night because there wasn't any hospital in East Chicago at that time.

Dr. Johnson was the first doctor we had. He said get all the ice bags that you could and put around him. We put him under this ice and he was just dying and screaming and screaming. So I called this other doctor, and oh, did he make a fuss. He said take all this ice out and take everything away. Wrap him up warm and put quilts around him. We turned his mattress over and got all the iron and hot bricks we could find and put him to bed as warm as we could make him. We let all the windows down. He had a fever at first. And then the fever broke; he got much better with all of the warmth.

His illness changed our wedding plans. We had wanted to have a church wedding, but Buddy wanted to see his sister get married. So we decided just to get married there at the house.

My uncle was there, and of course the sick brother, and Leroy. Lucille Tonsel was my bridesmaid. Roosevelt Newman was the best man and Boss Newman, his brother, was there also. There was about thirty people altogether.

I had a borrowed wedding dress. I borrowed this preacher's daughter's wedding dress. She got married a year before. When I was going to get married, she was going to have a baby and couldn't afford to give us a gift. So she let me wear her wedding dress as her gift. Then the dress that I had bought, which was a nice handmade dress, my bridesmaid wore.

And we was married.

Your Dad Was
Always Helping People

We moved into our own place, a four-room, two-bedroom apartment the same day. Mr. Comer had saved some money, and we went into Chicago to Hartman's Furniture Store and bought four rooms of brand-new furniture. We bought this icebox that would hold a hundred pounds of ice and that would last you two or three days. Many people had those little record players that set on a table. We had the better kind that set on the floor, and nobody else in the neighborhood had one like it.

There was no such thing as a radio. The record player was all you had. The only radio you got was to walk down the street. The radio was whatever people were talking about up and down the street. The first radio I ever heard was going down Michigan Avenue. Some workmen had this thing out in the street and had it talking. People were ganging around to hear it talk.

For two years after I got married I didn't work. I just took care of the house. We took his brother, his brother-in-law, and a cousin in with us—your Uncle John, Brother Hines, and Cousin Joe. They were living with Mr. Comer when we were married, you know, bunking together. He told them to get them a place because he was getting married and moving into this new home. But they didn't get any place; they just moved on in with him. He told them that after I got there it would be up to me whether I wanted to keep them. I had no complaints—they were very nice—so they stayed. Brother Hines had worked in the South—domestic work in the homes of rich white people and he knew how to keep house. He would make them get up and clean their own room and wash the dishes and so forth.

They thought the world and all of me. Brother Hines was more like the father of all of us. He was older and he just thought I was a wonderful girl that could cook and keep house and do the laundry. Hugh's brother, John, was about the same age I was. And Cousin Joe was around my husband's age. We had a lovely time there.

Hugh's relatives used to come up from the South and stay at our house until they got jobs. Your dad helped them. Everyone that came up would stay at our house, sometimes a month or so, sometimes longer. As soon as they would come in, he would take them out and introduce them to his boss and they were hired. Every one of them.

Some people weren't family people but were friends of the family. We would get out of our beds sometimes to give them a place to stay until they could make a few paydays and get out on their own. I see so many of them now. They appreciate the way we helped them out when they first came to town. Also my sisters came and stayed with us when they first got to town. That's the kind of life we lived.

Back then they could just come up from the South on Sunday and go out to the mill on Monday and be hired, especially if they were recommended. Your dad recommended many people. Some of the best living people in East Chicago now—he got them their first job. That's why they gave him such a beautiful break after he got ill, because they said he had paid his way. He had been the leader of so many black fellows coming into the mill.

Your dad was always helping people. Sometimes I thought he helped too much. That made him happy, so I went along with it. I was not that generous. But, of course, I was the one to take care of them at the house. Your dad worked every day and when these people were there, they worked different shifts. I had to make the meals for this one going out at three o'clock, another coming in at four o'clock—not to mention doing the laundry and all the rest. It was a lot of work. They didn't pay for their keep, so we didn't make anything off them. Just helping them. And of course, they were very nice.

I Was Quite a Bit Younger

I was quite a bit younger than your dad, a country girl, and I didn't know much. But I was a good listener and he was a good adviser. Things that I didn't know about because I wasn't raised in the same atmosphere, he taught to me.

He worked at Hubbard Steel, as it was called then. He was working there when I met him. And his boss took another job and took him with him to American Steel, which was right near us. They were only there for a little while—not even three months; they didn't even get off the roster at Hubbard Steel. The boss didn't like American. He took him back with him to Hubbard Steel. And that's where he worked practically all of our married life.

Even though I stayed home, I was working right on. What I would make off boarders paid the house rent and the grocery bill, and we would put up a little money. We started the first payday after we were married. We were able to put up like fifteen dollars. In those days people couldn't make ends meet, no less put up money. We weren't married but a little over a year before we started trying to look for a house to buy.

Let me give you an example of what Mr. Comer expected of me. When we first met I didn't know how to go to Chicago. Chicago was something in those days, not a lot of broke-down buildings as it is now. It was a beautiful city all over. But going from here to Chicago in them days was like going from here to London, England. After we were engaged to get married, he took me to Chicago.

All the way he was teaching me, pointing out this, telling me that. He showed me how to take the bus and streetcar. "You get the streetcar here, get off on the East Chicago side of town, then get the streetcar to the state line, then get off and take . . ." and so on. The next month I went to Chicago all alone just the way he taught me. Before I knew it, I was in downtown Chicago paying the bills.

And he would not just throw me out there, he supported me to do things on my own. When we first got married and went to pay bills, he never paid those bills. He would drive the car there, but I paid. He said, "I know how and I want you to know how." He never fussed or made fun of me, he just showed me how to do it.

He was a stern person. He didn't believe in fun when it was working time (but he had a lot of fun when it came to fun time). He couldn't take being a fellow laughing all the time, doing nothing that meant nothing, "If you make it, okay, if you don't make it, okay." He believed that if you want it, you have to go after it. And he went after it. But he did not run over people to get what he wanted. He was a fair man—too fair sometimes.

He was on time going to work in the mill for many, many years. One morning he was going to be late because his car stopped just before he got to the plant. He got out of the car and walked to the plant to tell his superintendent that his car had stopped. The superintendent said, "With your kind of record, I'll punch you in anyway. You go ahead and take care of the car and come back when you get it taken care of. Anybody with a record like yours should not be docked." That's how much he believed in being on time.

Getting Ahead

We bought a lot, not a house, the first year after we were married. There was a house that we wanted, but it was right across the street from the church. And being church people we figured we would be swamped with people from the church all the time. But I wasn't thinking about any lot. When he suggested buying these lots around the corner from our first place, I said, "That's nothing but a sand bed out there."

The sand beds were terrible; you could hardly get there. You stepped in sand up to your shoe tops.

"Yes, but the lots are cheap. We can build our own house and one of these days they are going to put streets out there."

He was a man of great vision. He would talk about things that were going to happen, and many years later I have seen them happen. Sure enough, we went on to build this house there and a few years later they put streets out there like he said.

We got a contractor from Chicago. There wasn't much to him. You couldn't count on him coming when he said. He borrowed so much money from us that by the time he got the house up we didn't owe him a dime. But with the help of my husband, when he come home from work, and his brother and friends, we got this house up. We had to make a loan from the bank to finish it up.

The company brought bricks and lumber to the site—as near as they could. Because it was a sand bed at the time, they couldn't get in close. And we had to bring them from there. I worked right along with the men. I carried many a brick and pieces of lumber. And I held the light many a night while your dad was laying the floors—we did most of the work ourselves.

When it come time to build a bungalow in back, the Depression was coming on. And Mr. Comer said instead of building this bungalow we want, let's put a duplex in the back now. We can still live here, and build a one-family house later.

Then the Depression came on in a big way. But we lived well during the Depression, compared to others. We had built these two duplexes that had our apartment, a garage, and two rental places in them. And we helped many, many people during the Depression because we was a little ahead.

Things were so reasonable—clothing, fuel and everything. People with any money at all could get ahead. The plant where Hugh worked kept only a few people working, and he was one of the few. He worked two or three days a week and was never off the payroll. His boss was Mr. Connelly. He was a wonderful person. Your dad was the only man in his group that had small children. He was being given more days than the other fellows were getting. They complained about it and he told them, "Comer is the only man in this group that has small children. I think you ought to be happy that he is working."

Mr. Comer always wanted to get ahead. Since there wasn't a store in that little neighborhood there, he thought that this would be a good way. First we opened it on the lot next door as a little ice cream parlor. But people would come in looking for other things. So we started a little line of groceries. That was, I'd say, 1932, about two years before you were born.

We done very well with this little store, but it was

awfully hard keeping a girl to help. And Mr. Comer was too kind. He didn't want to hurt anybody's feelings. If he could step around them, he would. He would give away too much. He loaned and they never paid back. Although he was a lovely husband and father, he also had this reach out for other people a little further than I thought he should.

Some of the people would run up bills of eighty to ninety dollars. In them days that was a lot of money. In the couple of units we had rented out we had several cases where people didn't pay. Some of the people didn't have it to pay and we let them stay on. And there were several that went away owing rent and big grocery bills. He kept letting them have groceries and I would tell him that if they don't pay their bill, just cut them off. But they'd come back with a sad story; they're going to pay next time and the next time. It ran into big money and then they'd quit and go other places. He was just too kind.

Louise

L ouise, Hugh's daughter from his first marriage, first came to visit us when we were married about two years, right after we finished building the duplex. When Mr. Comer sent for her he thought she was gonna come and live with us for good. I was so happy to have her. And she was happy to be there. She was a lovely little girl, seven years old. We bought beautiful clothes for her and started her to school.

Oh, she was just lovely, but she only stayed with us for about a year. Her grandmother wanted her back. This was her mother's mother. Hugh knew this grandmother and he didn't want any trouble with her. So he sent her back. She wasn't back there but about a year before the grandmother died and left her with a step-grandfather. (Louise's mother was dead long before her grandmother.) He wouldn't let her go. We had to get a lawyer.

Mr. Comer had to pay a thousand dollars, in them days. The step-grandfather had the two little girls. This other little girl was Louise's half sister, not Mr. Comer's child. Mr. Comer had been taking care of Louise all the time, but when the grandmother died and this step-grandfather came into the picture, he stopped sending money and tried to get the old man to let him have Louise. But he wouldn't. He claimed this was breaking them up. After the lawsuit and we took Louise, then he didn't want the other little girl. He gave her to some aunt or another. He didn't want either one, just what he could get.

When she came back she was a little bit different. This grandmother had just died and her half sister didn't want her to leave. And there had been a lot of fuss over the lawsuit. When she first came to live with us she was calling me Mama herself. When she came back she wasn't calling me Mama. She said her sister said she didn't have to say Mama and that she could call me by my name. I told her that she could not call me by my name, either say Mama or Mrs. Comer. So she said Mrs. Comer for a while and after that, Ma. Until today she calls me Ma.

I took day work because what he was making didn't cover what I wanted for a child, like a piano and music and books. I wanted to dress her nice. From the time we took Louise back the second time, when she was nine years old, I worked until the year before you were born. Mr. Comer didn't like it, but I could see it was helpful.

I was pretty strict on Louise. She had been raised by two grandparents who worked. So she hadn't had much supervision. The grandmother went to work at five o'clock in the morning and would leave these kids with a little food to take care of themselves. I tried to make her what I wanted to be because I didn't have the opportunity. I could see she had the ability and I was going to make it be.

When she came with me she'd have a certain time to get up, a time to eat, and so on. She could play, but I wouldn't allow her to run and rip. She would have to come in and study music, and then she would have to take a nap and her bath. She wasn't used to this kind of thing and rebelled. She didn't know at the time it was helpful to her.

She always wanted to teach school. When she was seven years old and had other kids come over to play, she always want to have school. She would be the teacher. She always was going to grow up and be a teacher and have this fabulous house (that she has today).

Whenever we went shopping, when most little kids would ask for candy, she would ask for crayons and paper tablets. At Christmas, at seven, we bought her the little blackboard that stood on legs. It had a show of animals on the top you turned on a reel of paper. It showed fish and bears and so forth, and it had their words there. It had all the alphabet letters and numbers up to ten. She would write them on the board. That's how she learned to write so well. She has the most beautiful handwriting now.

After we put her in school, I could work from eight to four. And by the time she'd get out of school I'm coming out of work. I'd always race to get home before she'd get home. It was only a couple of dollars a day, but it was a couple of dollars a day that paid the electric bill or the gas bill.

Louise started going to Washington Elementary School. I used to have to walk her to school everyday because the kids were cruel in those days. She dressed real nice. Black kids in them days were wearing their father's old coats and their daddy's pants tied around with a belt. She was wearing clothes that fit and caps and coats and hats like the better-off white kids were wearing. And her being just that one, kids would fight her.

She was always so tiny. When she was seven, people thought she was about three or four. For a long time I would have to walk her to school and meet her coming home from school until I just simply got tired of it. I hid in a church stairway—outdoors—going down to the basement. And she was coming, running, kids behind her. I had a big stick and I ran out and started lamming kids first one way and then the other. After that I didn't have no more trouble. I went to meet her after that several times, but I didn't have no more trouble with them. See, the kids thought she didn't have anybody to defend her, being one little child. And even the kids next door was the kids that would be fighting her. The kids didn't understand that this wasn't the way.

Louise did well in school from the beginning. She went to the same elementary school with many of the kids whose families I worked for. Louise was determined to show them that she was just as smart as they was. And she was—she could hold her own with any of them. They were the kids of doctors, lawyers, and politicians, most from the Park Addition, the ritzy area. No blacks lived out there. Blacks couldn't even swim in the pool then. But the kids treated her well. She had more trouble with some of the teachers than any of the kids. All of the teachers was white in them days. Some of them was just plain prejudiced.

I remember one incident about Louise coming home complaining that the teacher didn't call on her. The teacher would say, "Get your books out we're going to read. Mary Ann, Sally, recite." Then this child would call on the next and so on. There was only two blacks in that room at the time, out of maybe thirty children. And that was Louise and the little boy that would "play the monkey" for the teacher all the time. She would call on him. The choice was never Louise because she was black. The little white kids didn't call on her, and the teacher didn't make sure that she recited. This bothered her because she wanted to be a part of everything. Consequently, she would come home and complain to me about it.

They had this parent's visitation at night. Her father and I went to visit there, and we made a special effort to get into this teacher's class that night. And just as Louise said was the way she was doing. So as we were leaving, the parents would speak to the teacher. So I spoke to her and I said, "I enjoyed the class, but I would have liked to have seen Louise recite tonight." She just turned her head and didn't give me an answer at all.

What I did then was to buy the books that they had at school for her to have at home. Things were pretty tough for us and we couldn't really afford it, but I told her, "Now you can recite just as well as anyone else. Whatever lesson you know that is assigned for tomorrow, you study it this evening when you come home. Then when this white child gets up to recite, you just recite right along with them to yourself."

Mr. Comer backed me up, "Get it in your head. They can't take that away from you."

There was other black kids at Washington, but most of them were in an old wooden building just outside of the regular elementary school. They had a black teacher out there who didn't sound like she had as much education as me—she didn't do anything but yell and scream at the children. And the white teachers and children all shunned them like they had a disease.

What they did to get those black children out in that portable was to send notes home asking black parents if they wanted their children to have black teachers. Of course, most of them said yes, thinking that they meant in the regular school. They didn't send a note home to me about Louise or any other black folk they thought might raise a question. One day me and Dr. Smith's wife and a couple others stopped in there on visiting day. The children were out there with no coats, it was cold, just terrible. We talked to the principal about it but they did not make a change until this lawyer—lawyer Lenore—threatened right out in church to burn it down if they didn't close it down.

After they closed that portable down, they tried another trick a few years later. I was doing day work with Mrs. McDonald. She had Mrs. Stanton, the superintendent's wife, and several others there for coffee. I was down in the basement washing the clothes. They asked me to come up and have coffee with them. That was strange because they never asked me to have coffee with them before. They were talking about this and that, and finally they got to the question of whether I would like for Louise to be in an all-black school, to have all black teachers. I was caught off guard there for a minute, and I thought, and then I said, "No, I don't think so. I don't think we would have the same facilities and a band and all. I figure we'd get the leftovers." They were not too satisfied with my answer and they didn't ask me any more about it.

They were going to build a complete school for blacks. Some blacks who didn't understand what this was all about supported the idea, but most did not. But when they couldn't get the support, they finally built Columbus School what was in a mostly black neighborhood. That stopped most of the blacks from coming over to Washington Elementary School.

The prejudice was really something in those days. When Louise was about thirteen, they had a band at school. The music teacher, Mr. Norton, asked for girls to try out to make the band. Louise, like everything else, wanted to be a part of it. She was smart at anything she did. Louise and another black girl went for the tryout. We had bought a new piano for Louise, and this other little girl was taking drum lessons from a company.

They both went for this tryout and there was two or three days of selections. He selected forty white girls, and not Louise or this other black girl. She came home crying. I called the school and talked to them about it. Norton said that Louise didn't have an ear for music. So I argued along with him and he said, "Let her come back tomorrow and we'll give her another try."

She went back tomorrow and tomorrow, and both times she didn't have an ear for music. This really got me upset because we were giving Louise music lessons at the time, which was very strenuous on us. After talking and talking with him on the phone for a couple of times, I decided to go and face him face-to-face. So when I went he welcomed me in and I talked with him. So he said, "Louise just doesn't have an ear for music."

"I don't take that. Suppose I have her music teacher and a teacher from a music conservatory"—which I knew would cost me money, but I heard of this being done by the people I worked for—"and have all three of you go over this test with her."

This kind of shook him up because he didn't think that I knew anything about a thing like that. He said, "Well, that won't be necessary. Send her back tomorrow."

He didn't think I would follow it up. So tomorrow I sent her back and he still said she didn't have an ear for music. I went back to school and he said, "I'll tell you one thing about it, the problem is we don't have a chair (position) for Louise."

At this point I said to him, "Well, I'll pay for the people to come and have this test, and I'll pay for a chair for every room in this building if that's what it takes."

Then he was really shook up. "Well, I don't think that will be necessary. You let her come back tomorrow."

He accepted her.

After accepting her he then gave her the most difficult piece of music to play. She had to play a solo on the French horn. They put it in the paper—the way she played, it was so good. And it said it was the most difficult instrument in music to play a solo on. So then after that Louise was his first-seat person. When she finished school he wrote this beautiful script in her yearbook about what a beautiful person and outstanding job she did for him. I talked with him before he died. I happened to go in the hospital and I see him there. He wanted to go over all this, which he was too ill to do. But he was apologizing and telling me what a wonderful person Louise was.

Day Work

In those days they called it "day work." You work maybe today or two days, sometimes three for one person. At one time I was working for three to four persons a week. That was cleaning their whole house. I worked for Dr. and Mrs. McDonald maybe on a Monday. Maybe on Tuesdays I would go to Dr. Matthews. I would go to the Van Horns and do a day's work. The Van Horns was a house with three lawyers.

I patterned my life after things that I learned. So many people would just work and pay no attention to what's going on. I didn't just cook and clean. I worked with my eyes and ears open. I watched and listened to them and the way they lived. For me it was like going to school. I have no complaint about most because they were very beautiful people, willing to help and teach you along. I would ask them about this thing or that thing I would see them do.

Little helpful hints they had they would pass it on to me. As they shopped they would say, "Maggie, do you ever do this or that? We do it this way." Those women would also tell you how to know that you were getting a good deal and what sort of stores to go to. At the lawyers' house they would discuss the business right over the breakfast table. That's where they did the most talk together. After they would leave—she was a beautiful woman too—

she would sit down and have coffee with me and talk. "Well, Maggie if you ever get into a lawsuit or problem of any kind, handle it this way." Their main thing was you should never try to handle a case by yourself. Always see a lawyer.

I learned the cuts of meat at the Brissey's house. I worked for her when I was seventeen years old. She had this cookbook which I had never seen one before. It showed the pictures of the different cuts of meat, rump roast center cut, and chops and calf's liver and so on. So when I was shopping for myself I would go to the store and ask for that cut of meat. They were always surprised because, as a rule, our people would go in and say I want a dollar's worth of pork chops or a dollar's worth of this or that. They could get the best cut for the same money, but they didn't know any better.

I learned the advantage of buying good clothing. You might pay a few cents more, but it paid off in the end because it lasted and always looked good. I noticed people that bought from the cheaper stores, and my children's clothes outwore them two to one. I remember the shoes that I bought for my children. My children's feet never looked bad. I wanted that because I knew what happened to mine as a child, and I didn't want it to happen to my children. You only needed one pair a season. I know some of my neighbors would buy shoes two or three to every one pair my children had, and their feet never looked as good.

I learned a great deal from some of the people I worked for. But—well, there were problems.

In the tenth grade Louise won the posture contest of about one hundred girls. She was the only one black. They had all white judges. They didn't use any blacks because there wasn't any blacks in the school system at the time. I told you how tiny and cute she was. She wore cuban heel shoes and I dressed her up for the part.

(Louise got another award like that way back when she

was a little girl—in a spelling contest like the one they have today over the country. They spelled down to twenty girls in the finals. She was the only black, nineteen whites. She spelled those nineteen whites down and won.)

That night after the posture contest I was catering a party for this lady. It had been in the paper who won the contest and some of her guests had seen it. I went in to take something to the table, and one of the guests said to this other woman, "Did you see a little nigger girl won the posture contest?" Those women turned all colors. I heard the woman I was working for whisper, "Shh, that's her mother; that was Maggie's daughter."

I didn't say anything. I just acted like I didn't hear. But when I went back to the table everybody was quiet. They were looking at me. It really put a damper on the party. And I was sorry for that because this lady I was working for, Mrs. Forsberg, and I called ourselves very good friends. Before that incident it was, "Maggie, bring this or that." After that she didn't have me come in to the table much more.

I worked for another family, the Friedmans. They were very nice but they worked you awfully hard. I would eat at noon like for ten minutes.

One day I was working and I happened to see her getting my lunch ready after her son had had his. He left part of his soup, and she poured some more soup in there and called me in to lunch. I didn't eat the soup. Her daughter came in—she worked at the store and they took different lunch periods. She saw I didn't eat the soup and she wanted to know why. I told her that her mother just poured in some of Myron's soup and I don't eat after other people. Of course, that upset the whole family. They were very angry with their mother. Many, many years after that they were still trying to apologize to me.

One time my husband's two sisters and mother came to visit us), and I wanted to take off for the couple of weeks they were going to be visiting. So I sent a friend of mine to work in my place.

This lady I worked for said to this friend, "I hope you're going to be like Maggie. She doesn't take anything. She doesn't take my sheets and doesn't take this."

This friend, knowing what I had, said, "Maggie wouldn't have anything you have in this house. She has a new piano and she just furnished a house with new furniture."

When I went back, this woman was spouting tears. She said, "I think I insulted your friend."

I asked her how.

"I told her that you didn't take anything, and she said you wouldn't have anything that I have here."

"I wouldn't. I'm sorry that you thought that of her."

"You got a piano?"

"Yes."

She went on, you have this, you have that? After that she got so tight I quit working for her.

The same kind of thing happened when I worked for another woman, Mrs. Tucker, the beautician. Her husband had to be in a wheelchair all the time. He would be taken every morning to his shoestore and she would do hair. She and I just got along beautiful. We'd have coffee every morning and then I'd do up the house. She'd send me to the bank to take her evening's money and never missed a penny. Finally the banker's wife, someone I had worked for, came to get her hair done.

I was there cleaning and she said, just making conversation, "Oh Maggie, did you get your taxes paid? My husband told me that you were in the bank the other day."

I said, "Yes," kind of quiet. Because working like that I wasn't expected to own property.

The next morning I went and Mrs. Tucker was all sullen. Finally she said, "Maggie, this coffee can is very low. I thought you just opened it yesterday."

"I did."

"It looks like maybe a half cup of coffee was taken out of the can."

"The can comes like that when it sits on the shelf so long and has been handled about. They're not full. The weight is there but the can is not full."

She knew that. But this was because she was wondering how I could afford property. She seemed to think that I had taken coffee. I had to tell her that we didn't drink coffee at home—my husband never drinks coffee and I only drink it when I am out with someone else.

The next payday I told her, "Mrs. Tucker, I won't be back."

She got awfully nervous then. "What's wrong?"

"It seems that you're accusing me of taking coffee. The fact that you would think that I would take coffee, you might think that I would take something else. So you look good to see if you miss anything before I go. If you do, I want to pay you for it."

By this time I really didn't need to work. We had saved money from the beginning of our marriage, built two homes, and had this little store. And your dad worked throughout the Depression and I had worked right along from right after Louise came.

She said, "Oh no, nothing like that!"

She tried to talk me into staying but she couldn't. When I left, she said, "Don't tell Mrs. Jackson or any of those people that I know what I said about the coffee."

"Oh yes, I'll tell them. Mrs. Jackson got me to work for you."

Mrs. Jackson felt so bad when I told her. She really got on Mrs. Tucker, "Maggie works for us, takes care of our silver, takes care of the dishes, never breaks dishes . . . !" Oh, they felt terrible. I never met Mrs. Tucker again, but I understand that she felt awfully bad about it.

Race and Reason

We didn't go back home as much as some folks, but we went some. I had trouble with something about race almost every time I went South. I don't know how our people got along with that sort of thing.

One time we went into a drugstore where they had ice cream. A white woman with a little boy was sitting at the table having ice cream. I gave the storekeeper a ten-dollar bill, and he told us we would have to go outside and eat. We couldn't eat it in there. But he didn't give me my change. I paid my last change on the streetcar, so I know I had to give him a ten-dollar bill because I had no change to give him. So I asked him, "Will you give me my change, please?"

"I don't owe you any change."

"Oh yes, you do."

He and the white woman looked at me, and I said, "Yes sir, you owe me—I gave you a ten-dollar bill."

"No, you didn't."

"Well, that's all I had. I didn't have anything but a ten-dollar bill."

"You didn't have any ten-dollar bill. You can come on back here and take a look in the cash register."

I looked at this woman. She didn't say anything, but shook her head meaning, "No, don't go back." She just kept shaking her head and looking at me. I didn't know

74

what to do. I was dumbfounded standing there. Finally she said to him, "Give her her change. She gave you a ten-dollar bill." And just like that, he gave me my change. Whether she was his wife or what, I do not know.

I ran into almost the same problem in Columbus, Georgia. That was the first time Louise and I ever went to your dad's home. At the station I bought our ticket back. Her ticket was supposed to be fifteen dollars and mine was thirty dollars. He charged me five dollars too much. The people we was visiting was hurrying and when he gave me my change, I thought it was wrong, but I went on in a hurry with these people. I sat down and started counting when I got to the house. I'm not too much at education, but with my fingers I could beat some people with a pencil. And I said, "He charged me five dollars too much for those tickets." They didn't want to go back, so I said to myself, when we get the train back Friday morning I'm gonna check with him again and show him the tickets.

I went up to him. He knew. He looked at me and he knew I was different. He said, "Stand over there out of the way of the people buying tickets." So I stood over to the side—just stood there. So when everybody got through with the tickets he said, "Now, what do you want?"

"You didn't give me the right change the other day."

"How do you know?"

"I counted it after I got home."

"Who taught you how to count?"

It was almost five dollars, like four dollars and ninety cents. He reached down in the money drawer and he slapped a five-dollar bill at me and told me to get out of here.

You see, I wasn't used to that sort of thing, being in Chicago that long. They didn't want any trouble from me; our people were used to being cheated down there.

I remember another time, in Memphis, when I went into the store where my mother had been going. I said I wanted some center-cut ham, some center-cut pork chops, and a lean roast. He looked from under his eyes and said, "Where is your daughter from, Maude, Chicago?"

Sometimes they could go too far and their own folks would turn against them, particularly the well-to-do ones. I heard about this woman who worked for a wealthy white family. She went into a butcher store right after a black man had been lynched. The butcher asked her if she wanted a pound of the dead black man. Them folks got up in arms about that and they fired him.

Me and Mr. Comer felt pretty much the same about race—there is good and bad in every group. You don't dislike the good because of the bad. He used to say, don't take nothing off the white man. And don't "cut the fool" to get along with them. But don't go out of your way looking for trouble either. I heard him many times tell you fellows, "Don't let race stop you from doing whatever you want to do. Just prepare yourself, your time will come."

That meant work hard. He believed that because Americans was supposed to be Christians, they had to open up and give colored people a better deal. And if you worked hard, you'd be ready. He was a proud black man and he used to say, "Just give my people a chance." He used to tell you guys that you should be proud that you are black. And with talk like that at home you all got along well with black and white children. I remember a teacher telling me once that you all got along as well with some of the worst hoodlums in the school as you did with some of the best children. We liked that.

A Lovely Little Neighborhood

We lived in a lovely little neighborhood. Our street was only a block long, and cars very seldom turned in there unless it was people that lived there. And there wasn't many cars in those days.

We were very neighborly, not in and out of each other's door every day, but we did anything we could do to help each other. So when another person moved into that neighborhood, it rubbed off on him what this neighborhood was doing and they all just joined right in the same way. Most were black but some were white.

Let me tell you an example of what I mean by neighbors. We had a storm there once. It was just about dusk dark when the storm hit. The wind lifted the top off the Beggler house and set it down on the side of it. Mr. and Mrs. Beggler were two of the nicest people you would want to know, and they had four lovely girls. Every man in the neighborhood, white and black, ran to see what he could do. You would never see them all together at any other time, but those men got together and got that roof back on that house before bedtime. No charge, no nothing, just neighbors helping neighbors.

It was also a nice neighborhood for children, everybody was very watchful. I think I had about the only little children at that time. The neighbors would watch like they were theirs. You children could only go from one end of the block to the other. If you started off that block one of the neighbors would say, "Go back, you can't go there." So many times I went to check to see where you were and the neighbors were already checking.

The Fields girls, and the boys, were quite a bit of help to me with you all. They lived next door. And Mr. and Mrs. Fields was just wonderful, education-minded like us. Most of those ten children finished college, and them that didn't went some, or did well for themselves without going.

Donald was the youngest and he spent a lot of time with you guys. He was five years older than you and like a big brother. He taught you guys how to play baseball and football and all kinds of ball. We just loved him. It's a very sad story about his accident and death in the mill. He was trying to save other fellows and lost his life. From a little child he was always trying to help and be helpful.

There were more poor whites in our neighborhood than poor blacks. We sometimes gave food to some of them out of that little store when they didn't have anything to eat. Around the corner on another block there was an old flophouse where some of the poorest white folks in the city lived. Most of the blacks in our neighborhood worked and made a passable living.

Those white boys you all played with, the Danton boys, lived across the alley from us in a little frame shack like a garage. Their mother and father was young people, and he worked only part of the time. That young white woman didn't know anything about doing domestic work. They could hardly make it. It's like in the world today, there are still a lot of poor white folks. White folks tend to try to hide theirs more than the blacks. Blacks have been poor all the time, and know that is all that's expected of us. We don't try to cover up.

But there were different kinds of white folks in the neighborhood just like there were different kinds of blacks. Mr. Flickinger had a garage in the middle of the block. He made a nice place out of it—not like a junkyard. His trucks were all put in the building at night; they were never left on the street, except waiting to be parked. He kept the place nice and clean. He had a black girl in the office. He offered me that job at one time, but I wasn't able to take it. I think that all his drivers were white. Those men would come and stand and get their trucks, but I can't remember bad language being used, not in them days, not like they do nowadays. If they used bad language they were using it inside of the building. They respected the neighborhood.

Back in the Depression people had to help each other out. The Ruffs were Jewish people. They were very nice, but they were poor. She and I were very good friends, and I remember that Mrs. Ruff helped this little black boy learn to talk.

There was this lady with a large family, and she wasn't able to cope very well. One of the younger children took a long time to start walking and talking. The other children were quite a bit older and nobody ever talked to him. People thought he couldn't talk. The child would come in to Mrs. Ruff's store and just stand there. And when she asked him what he wanted, instead of saying candy or something he would just point to the counter and mumble. She would say to him, "Candy." He'd mumble something and she'd say again, "Candy." She would put her lips down where he could see them and say, "Candy." Finally he would make a noise like "candy." She said, "That child can talk." And every time he would come in the store, he'd get this talking lesson. Finally he started talking because he wanted that candy.

In the meantime, her daughter had a job at the plant. They didn't own a car. A black fellow in the neighborhood worked at this same plant. He took this Jewish girl back and forth at least for two years. What I am trying to say is that's how people ought to be able to live together and help each other. There was nothing between them. Everything was just smooth. It was just people helping people.

The Newmans lived on the corner, "Boss" Newman.

Hyman was his name. He and his brother, Roosevelt, were our very close friends from way back. Roosevelt and I were the same age. Roosevelt's girlfriend lived near Mr. Comer's home, and Roosevelt lived with his brother near my home. We used to date together quite often. When your father would come to church over here, he would bring Roosevelt's girlfriend. And me and Roosevelt would walk back and forth to church together. Roosevelt was the best man at our wedding.

"Boss" had a nice place there. The house was set way back, with a real nice lawn. At American Steel he and his brother both worked all during the Depression. When other folks couldn't get one day, they would get in five days. They were an outstanding family.

"Boss" made a lot of money loaning to other fellows. These guys threw their money away on payday, and then would be broke. "Boss" loaned money sometimes a quarter on a dollar. A lot of times he made more that way than his check came to. He would get people out of jail—people locked up overnight, not a serious crime. He would get up $50 and you would have to get up $50, that sort of thing. He got away with it in them days. Folks were not such crooks then, and not so vicious. Nowadays they'll knock you in the head to keep from paying the money back. One thing about it, if you ever borrowed money from him and didn't pay it back, you didn't get any more.

One person asked him a question about who he helped. He said it this way, "I'll help anyone that's trying to help themself. But now if you are just loafing and not trying to do anything, I'm not going to help you." He would see a man trying to buy a house and maybe he needed $200 or $300 for a month or so. If he knew you well he would let you have it, no interest or anything. He'd see you had children and were trying to make it. "Here, you can have it as long as you need it." But he'd see a fellow out there drunk after payday and the next day in need of money, he wouldn't give him a nickel, or would charge him heavy.

He tried to start a cab business there in town once. His sister, Mrs. Turner, she was in politics. The town had grown pretty big and there was this one little cab company. There was no competition so they didn't even measure what you paid. They charged whatever they wanted to, a dollar, dollar fifty, or whatever. It was getting pretty out of hand. So we were coming up to a mayor campaign, and different people were asking for different things. "Boss" and Roosevelt and Mrs. Turner and her husband asked for to be able to open a cab company. They wanted to start with three cabs, as I remember. So this man who was running for mayor promised them that if they got the folks to vote for him, they would be able to get this cab thing.

They were very popular: so goes the Newmans, so goes the neighborhood—they knew quite a few people in church and so forth. They kept asking, "Now when are you going to make this final?" This man went right up to the night before the election, and then he had to tell them that of course he didn't mean it in the first place. Because they were black, they could not get the license for the cab company.

The Hurds was another family on the block. Mr. Hurd was half black and half white. He passed for white in the steel mill. He was married several times, and one of the women he married was a white woman, a Polish girl.

She married this colored fellow, Mr. Hurd, because she was having such a bad time with this white boy she had been married to first. He left her and their child back there on the alley, dirt poor. Mr. Hurd's garage was right across the alley and they talked. His first wife had died. He gave her food because she was hungry, and he would try to help her like the rest of the neighbors did. Finally they got in love and they got married. But they took her little boy away from her because Hurd was black. The father wasn't able to take care of him, but his sister took the child because Mr. Hurd could not have him.

They lived real well—he bought her a fur coat and did

everything for her—and she was happy. Only thing was losing her little boy, that hurt her awfully bad. She took ill slightly. Nobody knew it was serious. The little white girl next door sat with her during the day. The girl went home to have her lunch. And she came back to see how she was doing and she came out and started hollering, "I can't wake Mrs. Hurd!"

We all ran there to try and help. I called Mr. Hurd at the plant. He came right away. But she was gone. She just went to sleep and never woke up. The doctor couldn't find anything. It said in the paper she died of Negro fright.

The Jacksons

The Jacksons was the closest friends that we had. We first met them in 1925 through a church convention. In a church convention, of course, they put people on a program to make ready for the next year, and it so happened they put Mr. Jackson and Mr. Comer on the same program committee. They had to get together during the year to work out whatever the program was. Mr. Jackson lived in Gary and we lived in East Chicago. So at the meeting they talked with each other and Mr. Jackson said, "Well now, you come over to my house and we'll go over this together."

Mr. Comer went to the house, and when he came back he told me that those people were really nice. "I told them to come over here sometime."

They had a car at the time and we didn't. So we were sitting on the porch one day, swinging, and we saw this car. It was very seldom a car came through. They were looking from the car to see where they were. They drove up near our house and stopped. They got out of the car and Mr. Comer said, "That's Jackson. That's the fellow I went to Gary to his house."

I remember I was cooking cabbage and ribs and cornbread, and dinner was about ready. I said to them, "Won't you have some dinner?"

They came on and had dinner and those were some of

the dearest friends over thirty years. We started exchanging dinners, Christmas and Thanksgiving. That started the same year that we met them, 1925. After you all were born, we started having Thanksgiving at their house and Christmas at our house. That's because we all liked to see you children open the gifts. We never missed a holiday all through that period—through snowstorms and everything, somehow we made it.

We went to so many outings together before you all were born. There was so many pictures we used to take, Kodaks we called them in them days. I look through the albums now—the men in straw hats and starched collars and us women in full dress. Those outings are the kind of things that we did for recreation at that time, going to Chicago to the aquarium, the museum, the zoo, and what have you. And then there would be things coming into Chicago like the Railroad Fair and the World's Fair.

When you were born I called them and told them to come over. We had this great big buggy and this new baby. They came and saw this big buggy. "What is this? Whose baby is this?" Your dad said, "That's our baby, that's my baby." They really couldn't believe it. I don't think they really believed it until that second.

We had a kind of competition going on too. When we first met them, we had a dining room and they didn't. They went back and they turned one of their bedrooms into a dining room. There was just the two of them and they had a four-room house so they could give up one bedroom. When they came back for the next holiday to our house we had built a duplex on the back. When we went to their house the next year they had pulled down their old house on the back and had built this beautiful brick bungalow on the front. After that we bought this big Buick car. And we came to their house and they had bought another car. She bought a fur coat one year and your dad bought me one the next. But it was a friendly thing, the way we raced. It gave you something to work for, to look forward to. Every year we tried to have something different to show them what we had done, and they would have something to show us.

Of course, the last thing was when we bought the house on Drummond Street. I called her and asked them to come over. And she asked what was the occasion. I told her to come to 3904 Drummond Street and I'd give her the directions. She said,"Well, what's happening?"

"Just come there, we'll see you."

"Is Louise getting married? What's going on?"

I wouldn't tell.

Sure enough, they came and got out of the car. They came on in and they couldn't believe, with all the children, here we are buying a house like this.

We talked about church when the other kind of people talked about the jail and crap games. We talked about what was going on in church—christenings, weddings, and so on. We enjoyed it no matter what it was. We had lots of other friends—people by for dinner and so forth—but none as close as the Jacksons.

Another Way

Some wealthy people were bad livers and some were good livers. Some poor people were good livers and some were bad livers. In our neighborhood most people were good livers, but some not so good.

One of your friends, Madison Turner, he didn't go to church. There was no timing or organization in his life. The time to eat was any time of day. His mother cooked and everybody go and get their own meal and go their own ways, even the small children. There was nobody sitting down at the table, no prayer or conversation around the table. He would get up and get out any time of day. A lot of people in them days lived like that.

Madison liked to play on our porch. He used to fight a lot and one of the rules of the porch was no fighting. So when he wanted to come upstairs he said, "Mrs. Comer, could I come upstairs? I'll be good and I'm going to go to Sunday School on Sunday."

Of course, he didn't go to church. But he was always a good boy when he was playing with you on the porch. He had to call me if there was a problem, not just fight. He always did and I would help you all work out whatever problem there was. But there were very few problems.

Madison was known as a troublemaker in school, and yet he was a bright boy and also he responded well when he was on our porch and playing with you boys. His problems stemmed from his family life. I don't think they sat and talked with the children or did anything together. He went his way and she went hers and the kids went theirs. The only time they talked to the children was to say, "Come here, sit there." But to sit down and talk with the children . . . no.

They were very nice people, but they lived like they were back in the South—sharecroppers. The house and surroundings didn't mean anything to them. It was very hard for us because we kept up our lawn and trees and shrubbery. Madison has been in and out of the mental place most of his life. I believe he's there now. He has a dozen or more children—really pitiful. I think his problem came from the home.

We had this other family that lived in our downstairs apartment that was the worst. Another fellow, his uncle, had lived there. He was very nice. He and his wife was a quiet couple. Her name was "Tiny" and she was tiny. There was a death in his family and some way because of this death he had to move out. He had paid his rent and he said he didn't want to ask your dad for the rent back. So he asked if his nephew could come move in on that rent.

We didn't know the nephew was being evicted. His truck came with this junk, and they stood in front of the door for three or four days before the uncle could get out. Later we figured out that they was sleeping in the truck until this uncle moved out. I told your dad there was something peculiar, but you know how he was. He would give anybody a chance. So the man moved in with three little boys and his wife. She was dumb as a doorknob.

I don't think they ever sat down to eat. The kids would be out in the yard playing and eating their food. She'd come out and call, "Tom, do you want some meat with your bread?" They knocked the table over and all of the dishes broke. They broke out windows—just tore up that apartment. You all couldn't go down those steps while those kids were there unless I was with you. And then I was afraid that one might sneak up—I didn't know what to expect.

They never paid any rent. They moved in on the uncle's month and didn't pay after that. They didn't seem to know what paying rent was all about. I don't know whether he worked or not. He would leave in the morning, but he was down there in the daytime. He must of come back or was just out looking for a job in the first place. He put me in the mind of my stepdad.

We had to have them evicted. When the people came and served the notice, he acted like he didn't know what it was all about. They gave him so many days to pay the rent. When they came back he was still sitting there. They asked if he was going to be out by nine o'clock or some time like that. They had a truck and they had brought three fellows from Whiting and they was ready to move them. When he wasn't out at the time they had said, them fellows went in the house and start to bringing the stuff out to the truck. This man just stood there and looked at them. When they brought it all out, the whole family got in this old piece of car and left. They didn't seem mad or nothing. And that's the last we seen of them.

You Was a Tumor

W had been told by some of the better doctors of the city that we would never have a child. And then after we had gone along so long, twelve years, the doctors was sure that you was a tumor. Dr. Boyd was the only one who thought there was a baby, and he took care of me through the pregnancy.

When you were born, it was quite an exciting time. It was like open house at our house because nobody wanted to believe it was a baby. We were very close to the church: Mr. Comer was a deacon and I was a missionary. So the Sunday after you was born, the house was like a church, because everybody from church had heard that there was a baby. Dr. Boyd and his wife was there. He was about the happiest doctor you had ever seen because he had gone over several doctors by saying there would be a baby. He'd never gone out on the limb in a case like that.

You was born during the Depression, 1934, rough Depression, but Mr. Comer was working some. We really didn't feel it that much because from the time we got married, we had started to look out for children. We were able to go along much further than so many people during the Depression because we had a little nest egg ready. So, once you arrived, we rushed out and bought everything for a baby. We hadn't bought anything before because people were telling me that there wouldn't be one. The only thing we had bought were little booties and under-shirts. We had to wrap you up in a little blanket to go shopping. We bought clothes and a big buggy, the first baby in the neighborhood to have one. In those days they had them with whitewall tires and it was very fancy. We took you to church in the buggy, all dolled up.

We was so proud of you. You know you have a big middle name, Pierpont. Pierpont Morgan at that time was the richest man in the world. You was named Pierpont after him. It was your Dad's idea. He always had high hopes for his children and he always hoped that you would someday be a rich man.

From there I had lots of tumors. Norman was born fourteen months later. Charles was seventeen months later than Norman. Thelma was twenty-one months later after Charles. And there was a baby, Ralph, after Thelma, but he died at birth.

You were all a little different. Norman was more of the rugged type than you. Like, when you were little, the minute you got out to play if you got your hands dirty, you had to be cleaned again. But Norman, the dirtier he got as a baby the better he liked it. That made him a rough and tumbler baby than you. But after a while you began to look and act like twins, so much so that when you were about eight and Norman was seven, some people couldn't tell whether you were twins or not unless they looked you right in the face. You looked like twins for quite a number of years, until you were about thirteen years old.

Some people were critical about the way I took care of my babies. I had worked for people that knew what this was all about. I had watched doctors. I had worked where there were nurses. I had helped to take care of their babies. The way I had helped to take care of wealthier babies was the way I wanted my babies taken care of. There was quite a bit of criticism about the different soaps, cosmetics, oils, and so forth that we used because our people in them days just didn't do that.

Quite a few times people would say, "She's spoiling them children. They have a bath twice a day!"

On summer mornings you got a bath, were dressed in your coveralls, and put out to play. Later on you took a bath and got your nap, then you put on dressier clothes for the evening. Many little children in those days got up out of bed and got out in the streets all day long—run in and eat something and run out again—and then at night would go to bed, sometimes clean and sometimes no. That's all the care they got. Of course, in the wintertime you were inside more. You got a bath in the morning and maybe only a wash-up in the evening.

After all those years of marriage with no children, it was really a pleasure to do all those things, along with some help we had during those days. Of course, help wasn't that expensive. I had two ladies in those five years. One was with us about three years, Eula Lewis, and the other was with us about two years, May Henderson. These two ladies were with us from the time you were a baby until you were five. After that I was able to carry on alone.

Mrs. Lewis was a wonderful person, and she loved children. She had come up from the South. She had an older boy and didn't have any work and didn't have relatives or anything of the kind to help her. She couldn't afford food at the time, and often they had their meals with us. And everytime she put on a pot of stew or soup, I would have her make enough to take home to her son. Later on she was hired by the state—during the Depression they were giving people work like that. She would still come out to see "her children"—she always called you all her children.

May Henderson was the other lady that worked for us. She was living in one of our apartments. Before May came to me she had worked for one of the wealthiest white families in East Chicago. They had a little grandchild born the same year as you. They had all sorts of maids and money and everything possible to have, but this child turned out to be deaf and dumb. They didn't realize this until she was about two years old. May would tell this woman about my children, how well they were doing, and this white woman brought her little girl over to see mine. All four of mine were all cleaned up and out in the evening playing and having a good time. She asked what I would charge her to bring her little girl over in the evenings to play with mine because she thought that might help her to understand better. But Mr. Comer was kind of reluctant to do that. He was afraid because you all were developing so well that instead of helping her this might drop you back. I know that doesn't sound right today, but folks back then didn't understand the cause of those kind of problems. We weren't sure that you all couldn't catch something.

It was sad. They had all that money and I could do more for mine without money than what she could do with hers. But that's how it is. That's a part of life.

A Way of Living

Raising a family is one of the beautifulest things I know
a woman or a man and wife can do. Have children
satisfied all the time—that's the deal. When I look back at
it now, it was a big deal. But then it was ordinary and it
was great.

I believe in talking with children, taking time with them,
taking them to places of interest, doing things together.
But everybody don't see it that way. Some people wish the
children off, and they don't bring the children in on any of
the things going on in the home. So if they don't bring the
children in when they are children at home, how are they
going to know when they go out?

That's what bothers me about so many of our people,
they don't talk to their kids. Of course, it's true of a lot of
whites too, but they've got the head so I worry about ours.
Parents get on a bus and flop down and just sit and stare.
But when kids are small, you can teach them a lot. You
can read these different advertisements on the ceiling and
point out different things. You can say, "Now that is
where Mazola Oil Company's plant is; that's Inland Steel;
this is the fire department right here; what do they do at
the fire department?" or what have you. Just be talking—
answering questions, making them think about things.
That's what's wrong with so many children today. Parents

only talk to themselves and never discuss things with the children.

Children see this thing and that thing and don't understand it. They ask Mom or Dad, "Why is this thing over here?" or "Why is this man standing here?" You explain to the child and they want to learn more. But you find children that's not talked to—they're very dull. Only thing they know is something they got out in the street, and they hear a lot of things that they shouldn't hear. But if you talk to them at home, they are able to discuss and thrash out things in the home, and this thing outside don't bother them much because they have heard what it was all about at home.

Many people the only time they talk to them is when they holler at them. "Get away from me, boy, I don't have time, I'm washing" or "I'm ironing," or they don't have a reason—just "Get away, I just don't want to be bothered; don't have time." "Go sit down, shut up." Now, shut up, that's a famous one.

I think children ought to be taught some of everything, but not just showered on them. Some people shower all types of life on children too heavily, when they're too young. If a little child goes out and hears something that you know is a little early for them to know, you can kind of tell them. "Well, Mama will explain it to you later on." And later on you know that the child has heard this because they brought it to you before. You pick out the way that you are going to put this to your child, and you put it to him gradually. If you shower it on them, sometimes it is frightening and sometimes it upsets the child because they are not able to cope with that.

Children have to learn how to handle themselves. I remember you at two. When people would come around, you were a nosy little fellow. But you were taught that you must speak, make them welcome, and then kind of disappear if it was adults and they didn't come to see you. You would go to your toys or something. It wasn't that you better do this or you better do that! It was understood what you were supposed to do. Now, if they are kids that came to see you, okay, you can stay around. It's your time and your visitors.

You also understood that there was certain distance for you to go to play. There were certain people you just didn't follow and certain places you just didn't go. That was one of the things that we were very strong about. If you are raising your children and you want to keep them in line, I don't think they should be allowed just to rip and run any time of the day or place—or taking things from anybody. That's how little children get taken advantage of.

I remember taking you to school at Kentucky State where Louise was graduating. You were going on five that September. We were in Louise's dorm, but you were a little fellow so you had to be in the dorm with us. And as you came down the hall you were the only little fellow around the place. All the girls would pick at you.

They would say, "Jim, come and have an apple, have a piece of candy." Or maybe, "Come on and go to my room."

You would say, "Wait, I have to go and ask my mother."

They thought that was the cutest thing. Of course, you were safe there, but that's the way you had been trained. It was just a good habit.

You have to start that sort of thing when children are very young. If not, after they get a little bit older and you say come on it's time for your bedtime, they won't listen. I never had that. You might say "Can I play a little longer" or "Can I do this or that?" But never a flat-out "No!" That was so for so many people in them days, and more nowadays. People ask me today, how did you do it? I can't tell them for sure. It was a feeling in me what was better. I had seen wealthier people, black and white, do some things that I don't think I would like. I thought to myself, "Now, if that was my child I don't think I would want him

to do that." And another time, "If that was my child I
think I would want that thing done" or "That's what I
want my child to have."

Some people accused me of treating you all like little
soldiers—too strict, keeping everything too perfect. Thelma's room couldn't be messed up 'cause hers was off the
living room. But you boys could mess up your room because it was toward the back. You could close your door
and just tumble in the beds or whatever. You had a little
hook that you used as a basketball hoop and you threw
knitted caps on it for the basket. You had all kinds of fun
in there, but not in the living room, dining room, or
kitchen, except on special occasions and then you would
have to clean up after. There is a time and a place to be
clean and work hard, and a time to let down and relax.

Because of the fun times we had with you, it made it
easier when we had to chastise you. You knew the chastise was for your sake. In that way we never had a lot
of trouble with you fellows like a lot of parents have,
especially today. You did very well in school without our
having to keep at you. But I spent a lot of time with you
from the time you were very young, and kept an interest in
your work all the way through.

Your dad was the same way. He worried more about my
getting things and you children getting things than about
himself. He didn't care much about clothes—just enough
to be decent. But he wanted us to have the best.

Your dad did not spend as much time with you because
he was busy in the church, fixing up around the house,
his garden. But he had plenty of interest in what was
going on with you guys and was in on everything through
me. And you just loved him. When you were outside in
the summertime and you saw him coming around the
corner of Gargas's coal yard, you all went running to meet
him. And then when we got a car you'd hear it coming,
and you'd all make it to the back door and down the steps.

You'd go running yelling, "Daddy, Daddy." And he'd catch you up in his arms.

My mother came to visit us one time. It was so different to our life as children. She would see you all run and meet your dad and jump in his arms and how he would hug you, she was just amazed. When your dad came home in the evening, that was the happiest time of the day.

He had this garden across the street. In the evening he would go to work in the garden, and you guys would get your little balls and bats and go off to play. One evening he said to you, "Bring a hoe and shovel out of the garage and come on over to the garden." You threw the little ball and bat down and dashed into the garage and picked up the hoe and shovel and brought it to him. You said, "I'm in a hurry, Daddy, I got to go."

"Go where? You should be here helping me to dig out more soil and make a bigger garden."

"Daddy, I'm sorry, but my living ain't under the ground."

He said to me, "Did you hear what that little rascal said? His living ain't under the ground. I wonder where it is?" If he was living today he would know what you meant: even as a child, saying your living wasn't under the ground. He would be proud.

Also, he liked to work around the property and fix things. It had to be done. At one time we had six apartments. He couldn't afford to pay to have it done, so he had to learn to do these things. There was work at all times to be done from one house to the other. He did the lawns and all the painting, whatever was to be done. I don't know whether he liked that, but it was necessary.

His biggest joy was his family. We would take you every Christmas holiday to see the sights in downtown Chicago. One time I had spent what I thought we could afford and you guys wanted a football. We were walking down State Street and I noticed you slowing up. I looked back and you were standing at the sports store window. Finally

your dad looked at me and you all walked in. When I
went back, I said, "What are you doing?"

"They want a football," he said. "I know we said that's
enough already, but I think we'll get it."

He had a real soft spot for you guys and you knew it.
One time you asked your daddy for a baseball glove and
he said he would see about it. It was an expensive glove,
so you could only have one for the three of you. You guys
started figuring out when you were going to use the glove,
talking about who would control it on certain days. I
overheard and I said, "He didn't say you were going to
get the glove. He said he'd see."

You all said, "But we know that whenever he says he'll
see, that means he is going to do it."

Four children was the beautifulest number to raise. Any
little time you could have a party with four children. The
days when the weather was bad, I would make cookies
and candies and you would just have a party. I used to
hear people say they were sorry the children were home,
out of school; they were in the way. It was really happy
days for me. When I knew you were going to be home, I
would get up and get my work done to be able to do these
things with you. People don't know that's the happiest
time of life when you have your young children around
you.

I used to read you all the Sunday funny paper when you
were just little bitty children. We got three different papers
on Sunday—the *Herald*, the *Times*, and the *Tribune*. There
was a funny paper with every one. I would read all the
papers to you at one time. We had a big chair where I'd
sit, and one would sit on one side on the arm of the chair
and one on the other and the other two on my knee or
down in front of me. And I would read this funny paper
to you.

After I had read it all, one would whisper to the other,
"Tell Mom to read this one for you." OK, I'd read this one
for him, and then the other would say, "Now, tell her to

read this one for you." And so you kept on until we would go over the papers a second time. But I enjoyed it. Those were the happy days.

I remember taking you to the lake—Lake Front Park. Your dad and I had so many of the same thoughts that it wasn't hard. Just about the time I'd be thinking about going to the park he'd say, "Let's take the children out to the park this evening." And I'd say, "Oh yes, I was just thinking about that."

At that time the lake front was beautiful, with beautiful homes. Only wealthy people could live out there. But it was a real nice place to go to spend an evening. When you were very small, we'd give you a nickel apiece to buy an ice cream cone while you were out there. Later on we were able to give you a little bit more—I remember that we were able to give you about a quarter; boy, you thought you were really in the money.

But when we gave you a quarter, you were going to spend a nickel and that other money you were going to put into your little bank. I bought each one a little bank. I remember some of the saying on the banks. Yours was, "Start with a coin and end with a barrel of money." Your bank was a little barrel. Charles's was a clock and it said, "It is time to save."

We wanted to have such things that children should have to be happy, but we couldn't afford it. So I did a lot of things on my own. I could make enough of whatever it was—ice cream or popsicles or popcorn—at home. You could make a whole pot of popcorn for a dime when you would have to pay a dime for one child's little bag of corn from the store. And it was more fun. The malted milks got to be famous. In them days it cost a dime or fifteen cents to buy one at the store. I thought about this and I bought a little malted milk machine. I sat it on the sink and made ice cream every weekend for the children to have all that they wanted to eat. Then I would pack a couple of trays with ice cream in the refrigerator. When you wanted some during the week you could drop a ball of ice cream from the refrigerator in milk and put malt in this machine and turn it on. This way I could make for four what I would pay for one in the store or someplace. And better, all four of you got to enjoy this together.

We were education-minded in your toys but also we wanted you to have fun. When we could we bought your toys with the alphabetics on them. We bought you a little chair that had the alphabetics written on the back. The table with it had alphabetics and the numbers. When you started to school, all of you, you knew your numbers up to 100 and the alphabetics. And the things that they taught in kingergarten, you helped the teacher teach it because you had gone through that at home.

Your favorite toy was your doctor's kit. When you were no more than two and Norman was the baby, he was ill and we had called the doctor to come in. The lady that was working for us said to you, "Don't do that, if you do I'm going to tell the doctor on you when he comes."

And you said, "I not afraid of doctors. When I get to be a big man I going to be a doctor."

Of course, I took you up on that, and after that we started buying a little doctor kit with all those little medicines, which was candy—that made two reasons why you liked to play with the kit, to act like a doctor and to eat candy. If any of us got a little scratch or anything of the kind, we'd say, "Come on, doc, and wrap my finger." Of course, we were laughed at for that. Some people would say, "Oh, you know he's never going to be a doctor. Why would you say that?" But we didn't pay attention to them. We just did things our own way. We kept talking up that doctor business, and naturally that's what you went for.

Yes, my life was you children. One time your dad figured I needed a rest. We got someone to stay with the kids and I took a day off down in Chicago, just to have dinner and mill around. The first thing I did was to shop for you guys. I said, "Oh, I think Jim would like this little thing

. . . and oh, Thelma would like these little dishes . . . clothing for this one."

I got home that evening and your dad was all smiling because I had a day off. I said, "Let me show you what I bought—this for Norman, this for Charles, this for Jimmy, this for Thelma." And he looked at me and said, "Now, what did you buy yourself?" I hadn't even bought a pair of hose for myself. But it was because this was my life.

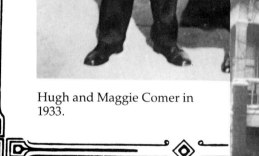

Hugh and Maggie Comer in 1933.

This is the house my mother and father built in 1933, with Louise in front. I was born here.

Mom, Cousin Mary, and me in 1935.

Church was the center of our family's life: this is the Zion Baptist Church congregation in 1935. I'm on Dad's knee (first child from right).

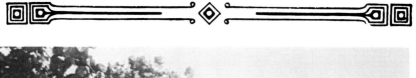

It was very seldom a car came through, but our long-time friend Thomas L. Jackson had one. Here it is, with Dad on the left and Mr. Jackson on the right.

Louise was the first of us to earn a degree. Here she is, holding me (June 1935).

With brothers Charles (left) and Norman (right), in 1941.

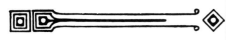

The four Comers (I'm the one with the tie) with Donald Fields, our next-door neighbor and "big brother," and Oscar Hall (in suspenders) in Donald's front yard.

Sister Thelma in her legendary white fur coat.

Norman, Charles, me, and Thelma, feeling very patriotic, in 1943.

The whole family together on Drummond Street, 1947 (above). and 1953 (below)

Dad, 1954, the year before he passed.

Our thirtieth consecutive Thanksgiving dinner with the Jacksons, 1955.

In high school, I found my
star in student government.
Here Charles, our friend
Carl Dahlin, and I present
the flag to our principal.

At mostly white Indiana
University, our fraternity had
the top academic average of all
fraternities on campus. Here we
are at the spring formal, 1953.
(I'm fifth from the left, front row.)

At predominantly black Howard
University, I was free of the need
to prove something every step of
the way. Here I am in 1959, in my
third year of medical school.

When Shirley Arnold and I married in 1959 in Crawfordsville, Indiana.

Mission accomplished; time to relax. This is Mom's passport photo for her first trip abroad with our family, 1970.

Working in the schools: I wanted to give low-income black children the same chance in life—through education—that I'd had. *(Photo: Marjorie Janis)*

Observing at Ruth Wilson's third-grade class at Martin Luther King, Jr., Elementary School, 1980. As a result of our program, the kids are now scoring dramatically above their former levels. *(Photo: Marjorie Janis)*

PART II

MY TURN

An Autobiography
by
James P. Comer

At Home

"Jimmy, Nor—man, Char—rles, Thelma!"

About seven o'clock on summer evenings Mom came out on the porch and summoned the flock in a voice that rolled through the neighborhood. Little Comers—me, eight years; Norman, seven; Charles, five; Thelma, four—appeared from everywhere. It was like a fire drill. No dillying or dallying. And no excuses—you were expected to come when called.

We lived on the second floor of a duplex at 1028 138th Place. We would sit on the front stairs with Mom or Louise and drink homemade malted milks. Sometimes Dad would sit with us on the front porch swing and we'd eat big bowls of homemade popcorn. The hot tamale man would come by: "Red hots, get your red hot tamales here!" The ice cream man on his tricycle would ring a little bell and usually draw a crowd. But not us. We had our own snacks.

We lived a half block from the railroad tracks behind the coal yard. A train roared by just before bedtime. Afterward, we'd say our prayers and scramble into bed. Mom and Dad slept in the bedroom, Thelma and Louise slept on foldaway beds in the dining room, and me, Norman, and Charles all slept on the foldout sofa in the living room—two heads at one end and one at the other. It was a little tight for the man in the middle.

105

*   *   *

Dad watered the grass every evening. As a child I thought he was very tall. Actually he was 5' 9". But he had a wiry, strong-looking build. I used to love to hold the hose with him. It made me feel big—and safe. But when I was big enough to water the grass by myself I didn't like doing it anymore. After a splash here and a splash there—and Mom or Dad insisting on more—I would point out that it was not necessary to soak it.

One day I was playing my toy slide trombone in the living room when the slide jammed. I went in the kitchen to get help and I knew immediately that something was very wrong. Instead of the usual lively conversation and dinnertime preparation, Mom, Dad, and Louise were all huddled around a small radio, looking glum. It was December 8, 1941.

"What's the matter," I asked?

I was told that Franklin Delano Roosevelt—*our* President— had just declared war on Japan because of the bombing of Pearl Harbor the day before. I didn't understand, but it didn't sound good. Mom put her arm around my shoulder and said, "It will be okay." With Mom, Dad, Louise, and *our* President taking care of it, I knew that it would be. I had been told that FDR was the first President since Lincoln who cared anything about our people.

During the war, all the kids in the neighborhood collected tin cans for recycling. In school each week we bought ten-cent stamps and pasted them in our books until we had enough to buy a war bond. The Christmas of 1942, me, Norman, and Charles got soldier suits and toy guns as presents. We went to visit Elray Johnson, who was a black second lieutenant home on Christmas leave. I loved that lieutenant bar on his shoulder, and I wanted one just like that when I grew up. Everybody was very proud of him because there were so few black officers in the Army.

*   *   *

In the spring of 1943 I had to get eyeglasses. I bet my brother Norman that he could not throw a rock from across the yard and break my glasses. Always willing to take a dare, he took aim and threw a rock. Ping! Bull's-eye— right in the middle of the glass over my right eye, my good eye. I could have been blinded. We got our behinds toasted for that stupidity. Norman later became a quarter-back on the high school football team. If I'd only known.

Mrs. Givens, who lived at the end of the block was my confidante. She always gave the same responses as my mother to the questions I raised.

"Everybody else can stay out later, why can't I?"

"Everybody doesn't live at your house, you do. Your mama and your papa are looking out for you."

And I thought, "If you all say so, it must make sense." I had no choice if it didn't.

Washington Elementary School

My fifth birthday was three weeks after the start of school. Mom had to entertain her club at our house that day, so she arranged to have a party for me at school. I loved being the birthday boy.

The next day one of my white classmates begged me to take a different route and walk by his house on the way home. His mother was hanging laundry on the back porch of their second-story apartment. He called up to her triumphantly, "Ma, this is the boy that had the party in school yesterday!"

The mother looked at me quizzically and said, "You didn't really have a birthday party, did you?" I indicated that I did. "Well!" she said. "It's the first time I ever heard of a nigger having any kind of a party but a drunken brawl." She turned and walked into the house. I was too young to fully understand. But I knew that she said something bad about me. I cried.

That incident was unusual. All four of us—me, Norman, Charles, Thelma—were occasionally invited to the birthday parties of our white classmates, and we were always treated well. I didn't tell mom what happened after my kindergarten party, but she was cautious anyway, and always called to make certain that the parents knew that we were black and to determine whether we were welcome or not.

At one birthday party the party boy's mother told us that we were all welcome and that she wanted us to all have a good time. I was the only black kid there, and she looked at me with a big smile and said, "And you too." The other kids appeared puzzled by the special recognition—I was one of the gang—but they dismissed the comment and kept going. I understood, felt a little uncomfortable, but also kept going. Being one of the gang was important to me, maybe no more than to any other kid, but maybe more. I still remember that when we exchanged valentine cards in the second grade I got seventeen—the second highest total in the class.

This was the same Washington Elementary School that my oldest sister Louise had gone to more than a decade before. It still served the highest-income group in our town, but now served a larger number of working-class white families. Because the black families lived at the fringe of the school district, there were only three other black students in kindergarten. The only black staff was the school janitor. But the school was a real part of the community and I felt like a part of the school.

I used to go shopping with my mother, father, brothers and sisters, at the A&P Store in the neighborhood every Friday. We would see somebody from our school there almost every time—Miss McFeeley, the principal, the school clerk, one or two teachers. "How are you?" "Fine." "How are you?" And, "How is Jim doing in school?" It was tough to do anything but behave properly and work hard when your parents were in contact with school people like that.

Mom never missed Parent Visitation Day. She was always well dressed and seemed to get along well with my teachers. Norman told me that he was glad Mom came because he noticed, as a little kid, that the kids whose parents came to school received more attention. Robert English, a black classmate of Norman's, said that he didn't want his mother in school because "she might embarrass me in front of these white folks."

There were occasional problems. Mom didn't sidestep them just to get along. Once I heard her on the telephone, talking calmly but forcefully to our principal.

"No, I don't teach my children to fight. I teach them not to fight."

(Pause.)

"I most certainly teach them to defend themselves— whatever way necessary. Even you admit that Norman didn't do anything to that boy. He was bigger and he was sitting on Norman's head. I would expect him to bite him, or do whatever else is necessary to get him off his head."

(Pause.)

"If there's a charge for the doctor bill, we'll pay it. But I don't expect my children to let anybody walk over them."

I was about nine at the time. And another incident from that period stands out in my memory. At that awkward age, there was nothing about me that resembled a swan, black or white. I wore thick glasses, had buck teeth—earning me, in 1943, the nickname "Hirohito." One day the gym coach had us going through calisthenics. I didn't perform very well. That weekend my friend Madison Turner was teasing me about having to duck-waddle as punishment. Mom overheard, connected the sore muscles I had with the punishment, and was ready to take on the coach on Monday morning. I was awkward, generally the last person chosen for gym class softball teams. Now I was going to be subjected to the ultimate embarrassment, my mother going to see the coach! But when Mom called on Monday morning she discovered that the coach had a heart attack over the weekend and died.

The rational side of me understood that it was a medical illness. But his death confirmed a small irrational side of me that said, "It's dangerous to take on Mom."

One year Charles got an unsatisfactory warning note— the infamous pink letter. Mom had the four of us in the car driving down Columbus Drive, then still the major way to get to Chicago, when she chose to deal with Charles about his poor performance. He had a special way with Mom and could provoke her far beyond her tolerance level with me and Norman.

She said, "You can do better than that!"

He knew that there must be a mistake but he said, "No, I can't."

"You can!"

"I can't."

"You can!"

"I can't."

Finally Mom got so frustrated she stopped the car in the middle of the street and said, "You can!!!"

Mom was not the best driver in the world—nor was Dad for that matter. I was always a bit nervous when we got in the car, although I always wanted to go. But this was more than that. We were stopped in the middle of Columbus Drive, the busiest street in town—right in front of the main fire station. Cars were whizzing by and I could imagine that at any second the fire engines would roar out of the station. I was terrified! I could have choked Charles. Tell her you can and get us out of here, I thought to myself!

As it turned out a mistake had been made. The teacher was new in the school and didn't know our family. There were only two black kids in the class. The unsatisfactory notice was intended for the other black student.

It appeared to me that good grades could save me from a lot of grief, at home and at school. Even my buddies from the neighborhood approved. The black kids walked toward our section of the school district together. When report cards came out, somebody would yell to somebody else, "The Comers got all A's again!" And the teasing would start—"That's why they got those big heads—headquarters. They have to store all them brains!"

Sometimes, though, academic excellence didn't help. I

used to arrange to pass by Mrs. Weldon's house, my third-grade teacher who lived about two blocks from school, just about the time she was leaving. We would walk hand in hand to school. We got a gold star for every library book we read, and before long I had the most gold stars of anybody in the class. Almost everybody else had read at least one book. But my three buddies, Rudy George, Nathan English, and Madison Turner, the three other black kids in our class, had read none. Mrs. Weldon was furious with them and lashed out in front of everybody: "If you three little colored boys can't be like the rest of us, you should not come to our school!" Her words stabbed me to the heart. This little colored boy never went by her house again.

The next year I became even more race-conscious. To correct an overcrowding problem at Columbus School, black students were transferred to Washington School for the fourth and fifth grades. One of the few blacks at Washington and well accepted there, I was in the middle of the adjustment process. My sister, Louise, had been a teacher of the black kids from Columbus; thus, they were my friends also. And my father frequently talked of "our people" —black people. So where did I stand?

In one class we selected a new set of officers on a weekly basis. After a while it was clear to me that the whites were choosing whites—except for me—and the blacks were being closed out. Impulsively I jumped to the floor and accused my white friends of doing so. When I sat down, it occurred to me that my white teacher might be upset. She sat in the back of the room and knitted while we carried out the mock government activities. I looked back to measure her reaction. She gave me a wink of approval. It reinforced what I learned at home: you are supposed to fight for what is right. I became the middle man–diplomat of peaceful relations. After that the white students began selecting some of the students from Columbus.

The real showdown came with Glen and Lincoln. Glen was a tough white kid, the brother of my friend, David, whom I walked to school with almost every day. Glen had established himself as the schoolyard bully. Lincoln was the toughest kid from the Columbus School. They had had two previous fights that year, one won by Glen and one by Lincoln. And finally the third was scheduled. The excitement swept the school. Everybody seemed to know about it except the principal and the teachers.

No direct racial incident caused the fight, but the black boys were on one side and the white boys on the other. Lincoln punished Glen badly, knocking him down three or four times. Suddenly, and unexpectedly, Glen dropped to one knee, his hands in a praying position, and begged Lincoln not to hit him again. The black kids cheered. The white kids turned away in embarrassment. I didn't like what I saw. Lincoln was my friend, but I didn't dislike Glen—he never bothered me. I didn't like the racial overtones.

Several of the black kids from Columbus were very smart, potentially as good academically as anybody in our class. During the summer between fifth and sixth grade I went to a Sunday School convention and Bible study class along with five of the best students from Columbus, all girls. Everybody expected me to make the highest score because I often did so in the public school. But in the Bible school class I had the lowest score. These girls didn't say anything at Washington School, and weren't generally thought of as good students. In retrospect, I believed they scored well in the Sunday School convention class because it was a place where they were accepted and relaxed. They were intimidated in the public school.

By this point it was crystal-clear to me that being a good student could save me from some of the indignities that my black friends experienced in school. The word was out. White equaled good and smart. Black equaled bad and dumb. If you were smart and black you might salvage a little. For this reason, being the best, being perfect, became very important—too important. Too many black students work under this pressure even today.

For example, in my science class in sixth grade I had twenty-four of the twenty-five questions on the test correct and I knew it. But I also knew the answer to the twenty-fifth, I just couldn't recall it. Finally, when the teacher wasn't looking, I looked in the book and got the answer. He caught me. He walked over, took my paper, tore it up, and gave me a zero. I stood up and my legs buckled, my throat went dry. It was the most embarrassing moment of my young life. I needed 100, I wanted to be first, I had to show that I wasn't dumb.

Sunday

One Sunday when I was eight, the family was gathered around the table in prayer. Dad asked God to bless the hands that prepared the food, the sick and the afflicted, the hungry and downtrodden, our enemies as well as our friends. He asked God to protect us from the seen and unseen dangers of life, to provide us with peace and prosperity, and the courage to stand up for right and justice. All the while the seductive aroma of the sausage, bacon, biscuits, and eggs made it difficult to wait. In frustration I nudged Norman; he nudged me back. I opened my eyes and we shared grimaces of impatience. Mom heard the rustling, gave me a withering glare, and closed her eyes again. It was like a dart—quick, deadly. Solemnity quickly returned to the occasion.

Dad finally said, "Amen," and we dug in. Norman and I later got a lecture about respect for our father. Sunday was his day.

Norman and I walked to Sunday School hand in hand with Dad. (Thelma and Charles came along later with Mom.) All the radios in the neighborhood were tuned to the same gospel station. We heard Mahalia Jackson and the Wings Over Jordan and the Five Blind Boys coming from the open doors of all the houses as we walked the three blocks to Drummond Street, the street the church was on.

Reverend Mitchell was the minister then. He was very

popular and the church was packed for eleven o'clock service. In the summertime it was hot and the windows were open, and everybody used hand fans provided by the Norman Dennis Funeral Home and the Nicholson Funeral Home. In the wintertime the radiators thumped. When the doors were opened after prayer to let people in, the worshipers streaming down the aisle, the choir singing, and the radiators thumping created a warm but almost martial atmosphere.

The four of us kids sat on the second row right behind Dad, who was sitting on the front row with the deacons. Mom sat across the aisle in the third row. She told me she had no particular reason for sitting there other than the fact that she just liked that seat. But the location allowed her to keep her eyes on the back of our necks.

One day after the service we got called on the carpet for giggling while the elderly ladies on the Mothers' bench were singing. In self-defense I argued that we didn't mean any harm, but that those ladies couldn't sing. "Why do they allow them to sing?"

Mom said, "You ought to show more respect. Some of those ladies were born in slavery!"

"Slavery? What's that?"

There was an ominous pause and then solemnly she said, "Slavery is when somebody else owns you and you have to work for them and do everything they tell you. And if you don't, they can beat you, sell you, or anything else they want to do to you."

"Who was in slavery?" I asked hesitantly.

"All of our people. You had to be strong to make it. That's why we're such strong people now."

I didn't ask any more questions. I was stunned. After that, not only did I give those ladies respect, I looked at them in awe. I didn't know how they survived something like that.

I didn't like the prayers as much as I liked the sermon. I got the feeling that some of the deacons were trying to outpray each other. If you didn't get in before the prayers you sometimes had to stand out in the vestibule an awful long time. But the sermons touched my eight-year-old soul. The cadence, the rhythm, the flair were exhilarating. The minister would gradually build to a high emotional pitch and then in a repetitive fashion give the congregation the message they had come for: "He's a Rock in a Weary Land! He's a Shelter in a Mighty Storm! He Rescued Daniel from the Lion's Den! He's a Father to the Fatherless! He's a Light in the Darkness! He's Eyes to the Blind and a Cane to the Cripple! He Brought the Children of Israel out of Bondage and He'll Take Care of You!!!"

"Amen," "Yes, Reverend," "Yes, Lord," "Yes, He will" rose from the congregation. At the peak of the service, an emotional tide broke open the dams of restraint. Tears came to the eyes of some of the men; women openly wept. Some of the women would shout and lurch back in the pews as if having a fit, their arms flailing back and forth. Two or three ushers would rush up to help them—fanning, patting them on the shoulder, whispering words of comfort. When I asked Mom and Dad why people were crying and shouting, the explanations I received always left me more curious than satisfied: "Well, Negroes have had it hard." "Some people have to let it all out." Later when I met some of these people in the steel mills and in the world beyond the church, I began to understand.

It seemed to me that some of the people got an awful lot of attention through shouting—and they shouted often. I noticed that the same small group of people shouted almost every Sunday. Everybody in the church was watching them, helping, concerned about them. Could it have been their Sunday in the sun? The official explanation at home was "Everybody is built differently."

At the benediction, every member of the congregation would take the hand of the person on each side and across rows, and we would sing, "God Be With Thee Until We Meet Again." I felt warm and protected at this time most of all. The service was then closed and the congregation broke into little groups of bubbly conversation as we all moved toward the doors. "How are you, Brother Charles?" "Lord, child, is that your boy? He sure has grown! Handsome young man."

But one Sunday the conversation was not so friendly after the benediction. Christenings took place just before the end of the eleven o'clock service. This particular Sunday the child of Marie Flood, a teenager, was christened. But the child was born out of wedlock—only his mother was present. Many felt that she had sinned and that the baby should not be christened in the church. Some felt that the child should not be punished for the mother's sin. After the benediction little groups stood in the aisle and argued their point. Most got out as fast as they could to avoid the controversy. At home Mom grumbled disapproval, Dad spoke of tolerance. They often disagreed— without being disagreeable.

After the eleven o'clock service we rushed home for Sunday dinner. Mom made rolls that were so light and fluffy they would melt in your mouth. As a skinny kid I could afford to eat six, eight, ten—and I did, and so did everybody else. So Mom had to make several pans of rolls each Sunday. And there was gravy and mashed potatoes, sometimes ham or fried chicken or roast chicken with stuffing or beef roast. Mom was an undisputed culinary genius. Sometimes David Boyd, our doctor's son, would have dinner with us when his mother and father were going out of town. He loved rolls and Mom had to put on an extra pan when he was coming.

Often someone from the church would come home for dinner. We stretched the table, but there was no need to stretch the food. There was always plenty. All of the kids always sat at the table and we all joined in the conversation. Mom always said the children are to be seen *and* heard, and we were definitely not to be left out on the food. She was determined that what happened to her would not happen to us. Every now and then Uncle Dan—no relation—would come and have Sunday dinner with us. He was a very elderly man and usually left a ring of food on the table and on the floor around his chair. We would laugh, and again we got a lesson on respect. Mom was big on respect.

Occasionally after church Mom would run by Granny's. She would take a basket of food to this woman, who despite what we called her, was not related to us. She was an elderly lady in the neighborhood whom various church people would look after from time to time. Granny was one of the people on the Mothers' bench until she got too weak to come to church.

Sometimes there was a three o'clock service, but usually we didn't go back until BYPU, Baptist Young People's Union. The major activity was the Bible drill. The adult caller would give the chapter and verse of a scripture in the Bible, and we young people had to find it. There were two teams competing against each other. Once Dad was the caller when Thelma was on one team and somebody whispered just before she gave the answer. Dad stopped the contest, "Wait just a minute, you can't be the winner, somebody told you the answer."

She thought, "Goodness, that's my father, even if somebody had told me the answer looks like he'd go along with it." But no way. Fairness was a big thing with Dad.

One Sunday evening I was going home alone from BYPU. I passed a store and out of the corner of my eye caught the glimpse of a drunken man standing against the side wall. He lurched forward. I was terror-stricken. I had prepared myself for such an occasion. After watching Westerns I walked down the street ready to take on any threat. But now in need, my courage failed me. I ran. But my legs didn't move fast enough. Morbid fantasy and terror was reaching its height when suddenly I saw a figure in the dark and recognized a familiar stride. It was Dad on his way to night service. I slowed to a relaxed trot so that he would not know that I had been scared. I was always glad to see Dad, but never more than at that moment.

From time to time church people from other parts of the state and country would come to conventions and special programs at our church. Many couldn't afford hotels, and even if they could have afforded them, hotels in our town did not admit blacks in the 1940s. Some of the visitors stayed with us. We slept on mats on the floor while they used our beds. It was like a party.

The real fun was during the religious holidays—Christmas and Easter. I enjoyed the spiritual side of Christmas *almost* as much as the toys and fun, even as a young child. The lyrics of the carols and songs—peace on earth, good will to men—touched a deep emotional chord in me. There always seemed to be a special peacefulness, forgiveness, and hope associated with Christmas. And I liked the idea of a little child a lot like me who came to save the world.

Easter had almost, but not quite, the same appeal. The persecution and the crucifixion of Christ had special significance in a black church. Even when the minister didn't tie it to the black experience directly, I could feel the resonance to the story in the congregation.

Church didn't end for Dad on Sunday night. He went to prayer meeting on Wednesday night. Also, Dad did a lot of praying at home—earnest, heartfelt praying. He prayed in the closet next to the bathroom, just behind the telephone in the hallway. I went to use the phone once and I overheard him praying in such a personal, sincere way that I thought he was on the phone, that he had a direct line. And in some ways I think he did.

Drummond Street

"Do you see that house? We are going to move there," said Mom. "But I want you to keep it a secret until all the papers are signed."

"Oh sure," I said, "I won't tell anybody." I went home with that precious information burning in my head. I couldn't take the heat and the next time we passed the house on the way to school I told Norman and Chuck, "We're going to move into that house. But don't tell anybody I told you, especially Mom."

"Oh no, we won't tell," they said.

When I got home that evening Mom said with a smile, "Can't keep a secret, huh?"

Our new house had two stories, our seven-room apartment downstairs, and two three-room rental apartments upstairs. We three boys had a double decker bed and a foldaway bed in our bedroom just off the kitchen. (Thelma had one bedroom up front and Louise had the other. Mom and Dad had the back bedroom.) The street was in a working-class neighborhood of family homes with neat, postage-stamp lawns. Only one other black family lived on the same block. Most of the men worked in the steel mills like my Dad, but it was a residential step up for us.

Some of the neighbors weren't as delighted about our move there as we were. A small group tried to get a court order to prevent us from moving there. The lady next door had her husband put nails in their fence—pounded half-way down—to discourage us from jumping into their yard.

We were given clear marching orders for the new neighborhood: leave them alone and they will leave you alone. Do not play with the little blonde girl next door. You have your own friends. (They were on Carey Street, the next street over, where most of the blacks lived.) If your ball goes over into their yard, ask for it politely if they are in the yard, but do not go into the yard after it. Stay off the neighbor's grass. Speak to the people who speak to you. And mind your own business.

Within two months the lady next door had her husband pound the nails down so that we would not get hurt. They returned balls that went over, told Mom how polite we were, and gave us permission to get the ball out of the yard when they weren't present. She and Mom became good neighbors. She took Mom's clothes off the clothesline when it looked like rain and Mom was away, and we returned the favor. But the first significant interaction came when she ran over to have Mom call the police because several visitors at their house got into a fight. Afterward I heard Mom say, "And we colored people are supposed to fight and tear up the neighborhood."

Mom and Dad hadn't bought the house because they wanted to live in a white neighborhood. But Dad had sat at the foot of our bed a number of nights at the old house, concerned about us three boys sleeping together in one bed. It was this concern that led him reluctantly to buy a house.

Every warm-weather holiday—Memorial Day, Fourth of July, Labor Day—Mom would barbecue ribs. She'd put a large tin tub upon bricks and place two large grills across the top. That made it possible to barbecue a large amount of meat at one time—and it was necessary because all of us and half the neighborhood had her preparing a slab for them. She started early in the morning and didn't finish until late afternoon. The aroma was intoxicating.

After several years of smelling the aroma, the white lady next door passed her plate over the fence for some of those tasty ribs, the same fence she once put nails in. Two or three more black families moved on our block in the next couple years, but it remained racially stable for about five or six years. Most of the first black families to move on the block were better educated and more upwardly mobile than the whites who were already there. As a result, the condition of the street improved. Katie Scruse, eventually the mother of "The Jacksons" (Michael) moved in down the street. John Dow, the superintendent of schools in New Haven, lived there several years. But one by one the white families moved away.

It was a great neighborhood. Nobody in my family lives there anymore, but whenever I visit I usually find an excuse to drive past our former house on Drummond Street. And although more people live in the same number of houses, the street still looks nice.

The Family Debate

The "family debate," budding at our previous house, blossomed and bloomed on Drummond Street. At the dinner table we were encouraged to talk about what went on in school or in the neighborhood. We didn't need much encouragement to talk—keeping the conversation orderly was the job. "One at a time, Charles had the floor first. Let him finish." After dinner these conversations often turned into debates. Mom often rested in the bottom bunk bed in the boys' bedroom as the debates got underway. Norman always took the opposition position. No matter what was said, he would disagree and challenge it. It could be a simple statement: "It's been a nice day."

"What is your evidence that it has been a nice day?"

"I got an 'A' on my English test." "The pork chops were delicious." "And the sunset was beautiful."

"What good is there in getting an A?" "Moslems don't eat pork." "And the sun has not yet set in China."

And we were off to the races. You could make the most outlandish, ridiculous statements as long as you could make them sound reasonable or logical in some way.

Usually Mom just listened. On one memorable occasion she challenged me. I was arguing that the public welfare system was destructive to people, that it should be eliminated. This was an odd position for me. At that point I was more often carrying the liberal position in the family. Nor-

124

man, more often conservative at that point, but for reasons of debate, was painting me as an irresponsible, coldhearted skinflint, and more. From the bottom bunk Mom said, "But Jim, how would the poor people take care of themselves?" I said that there should be a job for everybody and that the government should provide jobs when there weren't enough to go around. She said, "Okay," and said no more. That position took the sails out of Norman's argument too, and he switched the subject. I sometimes walked to school the next day thinking about what was said in yesterday's debate and how to counter it in the upcoming debate that evening.

One of the most onerous tasks of our childhood was carrying out the garbage. Occasionally Mom would forget whose turn it was. Being asked to carry the garbage out out of turn was a clear indication that she liked Chuck or Norman better than me. It was a cause for a complaint and procrastination. But she had a very clever way of getting the job done without getting into a struggle. She would often say on these and other occasions:

Whenever a task is set for you,
Don't idly sit and view it,
Or be content to wish it done,
Just go to work and do it!

She must have put something special on that "do it," because it has been rattling around in my memory banks, influencing my behavior, for the past forty years. She also used moral tales and demonstrations to deal with immature thoughts and behavior.

When we laughed at somebody else's ideas or ways, she would say something like this:

I met a little elf man once,
Down where the lilies grow,
I asked him why he was so small,

And why he did not grow,
He slightly frowned and with an eye,
He looked me through and through,
I'm just as big for me says he,
As you are big for you!

On the true meaning of Christianity, she told this story:
One day a lady got a message that God was coming to
dinner. The lady spent the whole day cleaning the house
and preparing the meal for God. She was interrupted by a
beggar who wanted a scrap of food, and she said, "Go
away, God is coming to visit me today." She said the same
to a handicapped man and a widow with children. Late in
the day when God had not arrived and the food was
getting cold, she called out to ask why God hadn't arrived.
And a voice came back, "Three times I visited you today,
and three times you turned me away."

Junior High

When I entered seventh grade in 1946, I was caught between two worlds—black and white. I was less confident than many about where I belonged. I had a lot of real-world growing up to do.

Most of my black friends lived on Carey Street, the next street over. And on Carey Street basketball was the name of the manhood game. In the empty lot between the street and the railroad tracks, we played basketball a lot. The way you became somebody was by putting the ball through that hoop.

I had a lot to overcome. I wasn't tall, didn't have much speed; all I had was heart. So sometimes I practiced all day long. One evening as I went back to practice, Mom expressed her concern with this obsession. "You're wasting your time. All colored people can dance, sing, play ball, and 'cut the fool. Why don't you do something worthwhile?" But that's exactly why I was out there. I was trying to be one of the boys. And I was already doing well in the books, the worthwhile area. She didn't have a case.

Of course, my dad rejoiced in any show of ability, academic or athletic. One day in a pickup football game in the alley behind our house, I went out for a pass. I went straight down the field, faked left, turned right, and caught the pass right over an open garbage can, disturbing the many flies feasting on rotting tomatoes. Dad was standing

127

at the back gate, and I looked back to get his reaction. He beamed with appreciation and pride like I was playing for the Chicago Bears. Anything constructive would get that kind of response from Dad. Unacceptable behavior didn't bring anger or a tongue-lashing, just a look of disappointment. The former would have been easier. The last thing I wanted to do was to disappoint my father.

While I was trying to establish myself among my black friends, a change was taking place with white friends. Close black and white social relationships were rare after the early teens, and I experienced some awkward separations. One evening I received a call from one of them, a girl in my seventh-grade class who was at a party at the home of another classmate. I suspect that she had been asked to call me as her penalty for losing in a party game. I had not been invited to the party and I was hurt. Mom hovered in the near distance listening, as she often did when we received calls at that age.

"Who was it?" she asked when I hung up. I didn't want to tell and wished she'd stay out of it. But she read my embarrassment, anger, and frustration. "Don't worry about them, you have your friends. You are just as good as they are."

On another occasion she made the same point even more strongly. One of the girls in my class told me, "My mother knows your mother." But then she was hesitant about telling me how they knew each other. Mom explained to me that she had worked for my classmate's mother years before. When she noted my uneasiness about this relationship she said, "Don't let that bother you. You're just as smart as she is. You're just as clean as she is. [Cleanliness was an important sign of goodness.] And you can do just as well as she can." She paused a second and added menacingly, "And you'd better!"

She kept a particular eye on my interest in and actions with girls. She had no problem with the hand-holding type. But when I was about fourteen three sexually active girls began to hang around. One day she spotted them at the backyard gate and ran out with a broom and shooed them away. Imagine a cool bean teen like me, and my mother shooing girls away—with a broom yet. Man, was I angry.

She didn't know about my experience with Dotty Flannery. Dotty was a full-figured white girl from the mountains of Tennessee, sixteen years old in class with us thirteen-year-olds. The boys in our class made advances of one kind or another, and she was flirtatious. For some reason she liked me. She lived on our block and she gave me a seductive greeting every day. Dotty's behavior made me nervous. My father had told me, my cousins from the South told me, all of the black women in my life told me, "Leave them alone. They're trouble, trouble, trouble."

She sat at the back and I sat at the front of the same row in our civics class. With the paper-correcting arrangement the teacher used, Dotty corrected my test paper. I did well on my own, but she changed my incorrect answers and gave me hundreds—and a big smile when I picked up the paper. I was nervous and confused about her behavior. It didn't add up—Dotty, a white from the South, and my hormones. When I told her that she was going to get caught, she just smiled and said, "No, I won't. Teacher won't know the difference." She gave me another big smile. She was awfully attractive. I was glad when that course was over.

Whenever I came home and complained about some minor unfairness, something another student got away with and I didn't, Mom would say, "Look, Johnny is white and he can do that and get away with it, but you can't. And besides, if Johnny jumped out of the second-story window, would you jump out of there behind him?" And on such occasions Dad would respond, "Don't let that bother you. The measure of a man is from here"—with his finger on his neck—"up," pointing to the top of his head. "They can't take that away from you." Sometimes he was more direct: "You can't be just as good as the white man to get the same thing. You must be better!"

At least in one case, though, I had gained a white friend who never changed. Just before the sixth-grade year ended, I was elected as one of the three councilmen to represent my four-fifths white class in seventh grade. The day after the election a handsome, blonde upperclassman, Ray Dahlin (he was Swedish by descent), introduced himself to me on the playground before school, congratulated me, and gave me a stick of chewing gum. After that for two or three weeks we talked almost every day before school. He then asked me to support a candidate he was backing for council secretary. In seventh grade blacks came in from other elementary schools, and I suspect that he felt that I would have their political support. I told him that I could not do that because a black woman who I knew better was running for council secretary. He was unhappy about my position, and I thought I had lost a potential friendship. But the next day he came back, as friendly as ever. He said that his father had told him that I was displaying loyalty to my friend and to my people, and "that's the kind of person that you can trust and should get to know as a friend." It started a close friendship with him and his family, and a close student-council collaboration all through high school.

Cultural Enrichment

Mom and Dad had this notion that there were fine things in life that kids should experience—educational places and activities, successful people going places and achieving great things. They felt that that would cause us to strive to do the same. That was their program. Mine at this age was to put the basketball through the hoop twenty-four hours a day. But we *had* to have this cultural enrichment. Some of it was not so bad. But piano lessons—in my neighborhood—ughh!

At first I enjoyed the piano. I got one gold star after another for my performance. But I was young, eight years old. By the time I was ten I hated that damn metronome I was supposed to keep up with—tick-tock, tick-tock.

Gradually basketball made it more and more difficult to concentrate on my piano playing. The stars went from gold to silver to red. But how could I get out when Mom wanted me to have this cultural enrichment? I developed a plan. Nobody expected any of the three males, among the thirty or so students, to win the piano recital. I made a deal with Mom: "If I win, I can quit." Fat chance! If anybody could win, it would be Norman. I practiced very hard and I won. Mom stuck by her agreement and I was allowed to quit.

Dad was always in church on Sunday, but when a friend of the family offered to take us down to the Field

131

Museum in Chicago one Sunday afternoon he permitted us to go. After that we went a number of times to the Field Museum, the aquarium, fairs, and a number of other educational programs in Chicago. The late 1940s were the early days of racial desegregation. Often we were the only blacks at these places. People would often turn and look at us; most usually smiled in approval. And to anybody who gave a show of disapproval, Mom gave a defiant glare: "We have as much right to be here as you do!" Though nothing was said to us about these situations, we too got the message!

Occasionally Dr. and Mrs. Boyd would invite the four of us over to play with their son David. Dr. Boyd was the first black man I knew who wore a white shirt and tie on weekdays. He was tall, husky, and soft-spoken. Mrs. Boyd was a handsome woman with a great deal of class. From the time we were very young children, Dr. Boyd never charged us for medical care because we wanted to go to college. It was his way of helping.

Mom prepared us carefully for such visits. And each time encouraged us to "speak up enough so that you'll be interesting, but don't tell all of your business." And if I came close to having any questions about medicine, "ask doctor about that," and I did. Dr. Boyd was a very important role model to me. I wanted to grow up and become a doctor just like him.

I sometimes resented Mom's pushing us up front and showing us off. Sometimes I'd push back, in a kid's way, without being fully aware of it. We stopped by the Boyds' house one evening when they were entertaining important-looking out-of-town guests. All four of us had to show our piano playing talent—Thelma, Charles, Norman, then me. They played well. I froze; I couldn't play anything. Mom was angry but didn't say another word about it. Half of me argued that I just couldn't do it, and the other half said, "Serves her right for showing me off." All of me felt guilty and awful, maybe even scared. Was it safe to cross Mom? Look at what happened to the coach who made me duck-waddle—he died!

Quicker, Stronger, and a Better Piano Player

Up until eighth grade Norman and I looked like two peas in a pod. By the time I was in eighth grade, my coordination had improved to the point that I made the class basketball team. As the seventh grade team Norman was on came on the floor, the Riley School coach objected, thinking that I had come back to play with the seventh grade team. But shortly after that Norman developed a ligament problem related to rapid growth. When he came out of the cast used to treat the problem he was three inches taller than me, quicker, stronger, and a better piano player. I had a problem.

There was a no-fighting policy in our house. "Brothers and sisters don't fight. They should help each other," Mom would say. She'd then tell a story of how her brothers and sisters all ganged up on somebody who bothered them unjustly. We did the same—to outsiders. But we fought each other out of Mom's sight.

On one occasion, unable to fight in the presence of Mom, Norman and Charles went down to the basement and had a silent fight. They came back upstairs dirty and disheveled. Mom said, "What happened to you two?"

"Nothing."

Mom started to say something and then she held back. They looked embarrassed. I think she thought they had had enough and just sent them to wash up. I saw a smile at the corner of her mouth. I could barely keep from laughing.

I won the fights when I was bigger. But now being smaller, fighting no longer made sense. I pointed out to Norman that we were too old for this. But he didn't always buy my logic.

He was a fierce competitor. One day we got into a fight during a basketball game on Carey Street. I gave him a run for his money but I was about to lose. Chuck had a lot to lose if Norman won. He wouldn't have big brother protection. So just before I was about to go down, he joined in on my side. Together, we controlled Norman. We walked the one block home with Chuck and I on each side and Norman in the middle, muttering, with the balance of power restored.

We loved athletics, but it cost a lot of money for Mom and Dad to pay for us to go to games. So we handed out programs to get in free, and eventually we became student managers for the football and basketball teams. I was the bat boy for the American Legion baseball team one summer when they played Gary Roosevelt, an all-black school. I was squeezed in on the backseat floor of the car behind the coach on the trip to Gary, the only black present. He couldn't see me and advised the pitcher to keep the ball down because if you throw a nigger a shoulder-high pitch he will kill it. The pitcher nudged him. He remembered I was in the car, and changed the subject.

Norman had a similar problem. A group of his sixth-grade friends started a pickup baseball team. Norman, Chuck, and Robert English were the only black kids on the team. The father of one of the kids arranged a game for them in Markstown, a section of East Chicago where no blacks lived. All the kids got T-shirts and caps and were told where to meet the next day, except the blacks. When Norman heard about the game from one of the white players, he assumed that somebody forgot to tell him. He was the best player on the team. He went to the pickup spot. They put all the white kids in the cars and drove away, leaving the black kids standing there. Frustrated and angry, Norman came home, got his bicycle, furiously rode through the most dangerous traffic area in town, stood on the sideline and booed his teammates.

Norman was becoming a fine athlete, and I learned the hard way. We used to play pitcher-catcher in the alley behind our house. One time, getting into the spirit of things, I told Norman to throw it as hard as he could. The ball came right down the middle and ripped into my chest before I could close my catcher's mitt. It knocked the wind out of me; we were both scared. It was the last time I stood in front of anything he was throwing.

Chuck was almost three years younger than me and was not a big threat in competition. But Norman never understood that younger brothers are not supposed to be better than their big brothers at everything. And he didn't even seem to try that hard. He just did his thing. The effort to stay ahead of my little brother wherever I could kept me scrambling. Fortunately, we were taught to be proud of each other, and we were: every good grade and victory was a family achievement. Thus, the competition never got out of hand and we were close then, and now. In fact, when he was in college and I was in medical school, he sent me a few dollars from his athletic scholarship to help me out.

One day after basketball practice we stopped in the drug store. I was about to make off with my favorite magazine while the owner wasn't looking, but an upperclassman saw me. We occasionally played basketball at their indoor gymnasium. It occurred to me that he might think that I would do the same thing at his house. I didn't really know or care about the store owner, but was it different? I put the magazine back. The concern about what somebody important to me thought about me stopped me from shoplifting. That is the way most adolescents develop the motivation to yield not to temptation.

Born Again?

Church was at the center of our family's life. There were no questions here about the status and place of black people like in school. When some of the people in our church "got religion" or were born again, they claimed to have had dramatic "call" experiences. Sometimes they would get up in church during testimonial time and describe them. One minister described how he was walking down a lonely country road when the Lord called his name, "Johnson . . . Johnson . . . I want you to preach my word!" He repeated the call from God several times, with dramatic tone changes and body gestures, prompting a chorus of "Amens," and "Preach, Reverend." One of the sisters in the church claimed that when she got religion she found herself running out of the cotton field singing the praises of God—buck naked. Mom commented wryly, "Maybe, but I wonder if something else didn't happen down in that field to cause that sister to run out buck naked."

Mom often privately challenged the message in the church. For instance, the sermon was often about the better world in heaven. She used to fuss about those better-day-in-heaven sermons. "We ought to be talking about getting together to do something about life on these cement streets we live on now rather than golden streets in heaven we don't know nothing about." One minister commented, "You must do as I say, not as I do." She said, "He must think I am a fool."

As a teenager I began to observe some tears in the fabric of the place of fairness, peace, and justice. A former tenant farmer family moved into the basement of a house next door to the church. They dressed slovenly, walked slowly, ate outdoors—and it wasn't a picnic—and tore up the property. There were seven or eight children in the family. They often had snotty noses, uncombed hair, bare feet and tattered clothing. But they were friendly kids. I sometimes talked and played briefly with them on my way to church.

One Sunday our minister got up and preached about the heathens next door. That didn't sound Christian to me. I thought that we ought to be helping them rather than criticizing them. As far as I know, nobody from our church extended them the hand of fellowship.

Another event shook my commitment to formal religion. Most of our ministers were caring, committed Christian men. But one of them was a charlatan. He overcharged the church for trips he took, diverted money from church projects to his own pocket, and had an eye for the sisters, eventually running away with a choir member, the wife of a church member. Early on Dad, as a deacon, counseled the minister privately. He tried to buy Dad's silence. Imagine that! When he couldn't, he called him a fool in a deacon's meeting. Other deacons had to separate them.

Finally Dad had to inform the entire congregation. As Dad described what was going on, the minister tried to start the music usually played during dues collection. The pianist started to play and then stopped. A few of the members went up to the front table to pay their dues, but most didn't. One of my classmates leaned over and said, "Why don't you tell your old daddy to shut up?"

A sister next to her said, "You shut up. Brother Comer is standing for what is right. You must always stand for what is right!"

A part of me was embarrassed, but I was also very proud of Dad—standing for what was right! The minister was dismissed at the next church meeting.

For these reasons my "call" and rebirth was less dramatic. The truth is, I claimed to have gotten religion in order to please my father. Our church had a baptismal pool just behind the pulpit. One Sunday morning the curtains concealing the pool were pulled, and I was dipped in the water and born again. Despite my doubts, though, it was a time of deep satisfaction. The younger children held me in awe. I acquired an added measure of respect from my age peers. And the adults were very pleased. I belonged even if I didn't completely believe.

When we were younger we were not allowed to talk about the bad behavior of other people. "We don't gossip," Mom often said. But as I reached the late preteens and early teens I began to enter bad behavior by church people, especially the cliques, into our debates. Mom and Dad pointed out that that was the behavior of hypocrites. Dislike and the bad treatment of black people and other people because of their race by "Christians" was often discussed as a prime example of hypocrisy. Gradually we began to ask Dad questions like, "How could one God see over all the people on earth?" At first Mom tried to stop us—it was disrespectful. But Dad encouraged us. He answered in terms of the superhuman . . . spirit . . . faith.

I continued, and continue, to value the message of Christianity, but I became increasingly wary of people who talked a Christian game and played an unchristian game. Gradually we moved from our usual seat on the second row to the middle and then to the back of the church. Sensing what was happening, the minister preached to and about me and Norman one Sunday, without mentioning our names. By that time I was a premed student and Norman was a high school football star. His sermon spoke of the great doctor who could save all of his patients: "But in his dying hours, he needed God!" And he spoke of the great football star who could run up and down the field, over all of his opponents: "But in his dying hour, he needed God!"

Our concern was not with Christian principles. We understood some of the needs the church met. For example, many of the sermons and signs around the church were designed to make people feel good about themselves. A sign in the vestibule said, "The best people in all the world pass through these doors." Our concern was with the way individual and institutional needs were put ahead of Christian principles.

Dad's Illness

A couple years after we were in our new house, I heard Dad coming up from the basement. He stopped every step to rest. He wheezed loudly with every breath. I was terrified. I was afraid that the next breath would be his last, or that he would fall. I wanted to go and help him. But Dad was a proud man. So I stood just inside the kitchen door where he couldn't see me, but close enough to rush out if necessary. When it was certain that he was going to make it, I moved away from the door so as not to embarrass him.

In those days coal for the furnace was dumped in front of the house. Again, as Dad exerted himself moving the coal back to the window of the bin, I heard the labored breathing. Norman, Charles, and I helped. Even Thelma carried a coal or two. I knew something was wrong, but I didn't want to think about it. Nobody else talked about it either, but in retrospect he knew that he was sick before we moved. He just carried on, did what he had to do, despite a gradually worsening respiratory illness. Dad was a remarkable guy—solid, responsible, caring, and tough. He was going to take care of his family even if it killed him.

And nobody pushed him around, even after he was sick. Once in the steel mill a young "dude" from Chicago who worked in the janitor's gang under Dad's supervision attacked him with a knife. Despite his poor health, Dad disarmed him with a chair and other workers had to pull him off of the young man.

When the young worker brought a grievance the union steward laughed at him, pointing out that he couldn't possibly win a case against Comer. Dad had worked very hard for many years. He was never late and never absent for twenty-five years. On the one occasion that he had car trouble near the plant, he walked there to be on time, punched in, and was allowed to go back and take care of his car. He had a rock-solid reputation for treating others fairly and with respect. The young man who brought the grievance was fired.

By the late 1940s Mom and Dad had come a long way. The steel mill had given us a small piece of the American dream that the cotton fields could not. Nonetheless, we were a long way from the dream Mom had envisioned when she was a barefoot girl in Memphis. Until now it had appeared that achieving her goals was just a matter of time. But Mom knew that the dream was in trouble, and she began to try to get a job in the steel mill.

One evening, Thelma, then seven years old, came home from school and rang the doorbell. Nobody answered. Mom was out interviewing for a job and Dad was in the bathtub. It was difficult for him to move quickly. By the time he got out of the tub and got to the door, Thelma had decided that nobody was home. That had never happened before. She began to cry. Dad had not wanted Mom to work in the first place because he wanted her to be there when we arrived home from school. When he looked out of the window and saw Thelma crying, he insisted that Mom not work. That was 1946.

As sick as he was, Dad carried on all his activities. Mom was always concerned about the large amount of time he gave to church work. Now her concerns, abetted by her deeper fears, turned to desperate complaints: "You are going to kill yourself. Who's going to look after your family after you're gone? They are using you." One time Dad brought home the communion glasses for Mom to clean. Frustrated because she couldn't get him to decrease his church work, she shoved him as she aggressively pushed the tray back toward him. He shoved her back. That had never happened before. She was so upset she had to leave the house. Charles observed the incident and stood anxiously by the door as she left. Although very upset, she whispered to him, "I'll be back."

Every effort was made to help Dad hold the job. His foreman told him that all he had to do was show up and punch the time clock. But finally, in 1949, he had to leave the steel mill. He had severe emphysema as a result of the heat, smoke, and dust he had worked in over the years. Not only did the black workers not get the cleaner jobs— welder, machinist, and so on—they often didn't get reasonable settlements for job-related health problems. But Dad received one of the best settlements of that time, ten thousand dollars. The money was used to pay off the mortgage on Drummond Street, and the two houses on 138th Place were eventually sold. That money was set aside for our education and for us to live on. But it couldn't go far without an income.

A family friend at the welfare department told Mom that she could arrange for us to get on public welfare even though we didn't qualify. Mom didn't like the idea, but she had a family meeting—while Dad wasn't home—and asked us what we thought about it. We were angrily opposed. We didn't want anything from anybody else until we couldn't possibly make it ourselves.

Mom and her sister, Aunt Seretha, worked from time to time for a black caterer in Chicago. Mom brought leftovers home—food enough for several days. (It was fancy food. I had cavier before some of the wealthy kids had it.) Also Mom worked on the election polls, at the swimming pool in the summertime—little jobs here and there. And we all had jobs—me on a fruit truck, later an after-school job at

Max Blumenfeld's jewelry store, and Norman took a fruit truck job. Charles and Thelma got political patronage jobs handing out baskets at the swimming pool. The money was largely used to buy school clothing.

Dr. Payne, Dad's doctor, felt that he would get along better in Arizona. Because we were well established in school, it was decided that we would remain in East Chicago and he would live out there most of the year. Louise bought a small two-family house in Phoenix, one apartment for rental and the other for Dad. Mom visited for a couple months one or two times a year, and Louise took care of us at home during these periods. I was fourteen the year he moved to Arizona. He lived most of the next five years out there.

Mom and Dad never talked about a change in plans. We were going to college. Dad said, "Just get out there and the Lord will make a way." Or, "Just get your head in the door and you'll make it." Without talking about it, without even fully acknowledging the crisis, we kids had all decided that one way or another, we were going to make it.

We missed Dad terribly. I couldn't wait on the days he was coming home from Arizona. I'd run all the way home from school. Thelma and Louise visited him out there the one summer he didn't come home. And he kept up with our activities through the information Mom brought out when she visited. But we had been a close family, and the separation was tough.

High School

I was singing up a storm in my eighth grade music class, trying to make choral club as a freshman. Our high school had one of the best choral clubs in the state. A black classmate told me, "Don't bother. They only take two Negroes a year, and they will both be upperclassmen." Mom always said, "Do your best in whatever you're doing so they will not have an excuse to turn you down." I was admitted to the choral club as a freshman. The choral club was fully racially integrated by the time I was a senior. And I was elected president of the organization.

My coordination was vastly improved by the time I was a freshman. I developed into a good basketball player, but I was 5' 5" and 118 pounds as a senior. (When I was a freshman I used to pray that I would grow three inches each summer for three years, or develop great leaping ability, but no such luck.) And although basketball remained my game, I had to look elsewhere for my star. It was in student government.

I was elected to the student council for all six years. I was student-council president my sophomore year and student manager (the equivalent of student body president) in my senior year. We had a significant family voting block on the council the year I was elected council president, 1949—Thelma representing seventh grade; Charles, eighth grade; Norman, ninth grade; and me, tenth—four of eighteen council members.

There was never any serious black-white student conflict throughout my high school years. The white students supported racial integration in most areas, but not all. Our recreation was separate. For example, as the seventh-grade student council representative, I had objected to segregated swimming pool hours, all of the blacks on Friday after whites had used the pool all week long. The mostly white council members passed a resolution against segregated swimming, but over the summer a floor was laid over the pool and it was turned into a basketball court. By the same token, the student council sponsored a dance open to all students to rev up school spirit. The opposition of some highly vocal and popular white students limited ticket sales, and the dance had to be cancelled. The issue was interracial dancing and dating.

Like some students, some of the faculty were struggling with racist attitudes. When I was elected student-body president, Mildred Steel, the biology teacher, said in class, "It's just not right that a minority should represent the majority." Norman was in her class at the time and she took her feelings out on him. She gave him a C, the only grade other than an A he received in a core subject all the way through high school. Norman didn't tell Mom or Dad about it. They were both in Arizona at the time. Without talking with each other, we had all decided to keep down the number of problems they had to deal with. Norman was a star football, basketball, track, and baseball player and a straight-A student. That semester, because of his talent as a bassoonist, he was the subject of a feature article in *The Hammond Times*. His response to her C was "I didn't need her grade to tell me what I could do."

One of my responsibilities as the student-government president was to appoint all the members of the various student committees. An exception was the lost-and-found committee: Miss Tower, the supervisor, needed to appoint students who would actually show up to provide the service. But I noticed that there were never any blacks on the lost-and-found committee, and I asked her about this. She told me that she couldn't find anybody responsible. I could have given her a number of names right on the spot, but I decided to make a point. I asked her if she would put a black on the committee if I found someone that she could count on. She agreed to do so. I returned with my sister Thelma, a highly responsible honor student. Miss Tower stammered and stuttered and appointed her to the committee.

Those incidents stand out, though, because they were the exceptions—painful, irrational, leaving indelible impressions—but still exceptions. Most of our white teachers were on our side. And some of them took every occasion to sing our academic praises. In retrospect I understand that they were trying to counter stereotypes among some of their colleagues and in the community.

I finished high school in the top three percent of a three-hundred-plus class. Mom and Dad were very proud of my high school accomplishments, especially Mom. I was the first of her birth children to finish high school. There had never been any question that the next step—although there had been almost no direct discussion about it—was college.

Continental Steel

The thing that stood between me and a college education was money. Although Mom and Dad were prepared to use their small savings, about $10,000, to send us to college, there were four of us. We needed to earn as much as we possibly could. I was earning $10 a week working part-time at Max Blumfeld's jewelry store when I could have earned a thousand dollars during the summer in the steel mills, about what I would need for a year in college. But I was only seventeen years old when I finished high school. According to the rules, you had to be eighteen before you could work in the steel mills.

A week into the summer, I was on a lunch break when I met a former classmate. He was seventeen years old and he was working in the same steel mill Dad had worked in, Continental. As soon as he left, I called Mom. Mom called the steel mill, and the personnel officer repeated the rule and expressed his sympathy. Mom asked, "What would you say if I told you that I know that you have a boy out there who is seventeen years old?"

He paused and said, "Well uh . . . well uh. . . ." Finally he said, "But his father works here."

"That's all the more reason Jim should have a job there. Jim's father gave his health and his life to your company. He wants his boy to go to college, and we can't afford to send him without his working."

I was hired the next day.

I was not ready for the reception I received. I knew that these were tough steel mill workers and I was apprehensive. I rode to work with Mr. Morris, a man from our neighborhood and a deacon at our church. As soon as we entered the gate, he began to introduce me as Hugh Comer's son. We had to walk down a long corridor between two main buildings. The word spread that I was there, and a reception line formed almost the entire way. All of those tough guys wanted to shake hands with Comer's son. They all wanted to know how Dad was doing.

One man ignored me. He was Joe Ricco, a supervisor of one of the labor gangs. He was Italian and built like the stump of a wide oak tree. Some of the guys described him as a tough, no-nonsense man, so I assumed he just didn't go for all that sentimentality. But a few days later he came up to me and said, "You're Hugh Comer's son?" He threw his arms around me, hugging, patting me on the back. He explained that he thought they were saying Joe Carter's son. He kept saying, "Hugh Comer, Hugh Comer—great man, you fadder, great man." I was amazed: tough, mean Joe Ricco loved Hugh Comer.

As I walked through the foundry, I met many of the men I knew from church. They were the leaders of my world—deacons, usher board members, trustees, choir members. I knew them in white shirts and ties, robes and roles of dignity. I was shocked to see most of them covered in soot, grime, and grease from head to toe. I stopped where Deacon McCorkle worked. Covered in grime, with dust, heat, and smoke all around, he explained to me that he had worked with my dad on that very job for many years.

I walked past a furnace with blazing heat and molten steel. I saw a black man with broad shoulders and taut muscles, sweat pouring off his body, straining to perform an operation at the furnace. When he stopped, I realized that it was my cousin, Johnny Lee. He was one of the people who had come up from the South whom my Dad helped to get a "good job" at the steel mill. Seeing what the important people in my life did to earn a living was a sobering experience.

None of the black men had clean jobs. Dad had once told me that he and several others had asked to have black men work in the machine shop. They were told that every time they had ever given a black man a good job, he messed up. Dad pointed out to me that that was a favorite trick—select somebody you know is going to mess up and then use his behavior to justify not giving such a job to a responsible black person.

They didn't know what to do with me in the steel mill. Most of the first day I did make-work. I swept the entry yard. That afternoon I was asked to help unload a truck of bricks. I did the same thing for the next three days. Those bricks almost broke my butt. I was as sore as I have ever been. I wasn't going to tell anybody that I couldn't cut it, and yet just before breaktime and quitting time I was an instant away from saying uncle. At night I ate dinner, soaked my aching muscles in the tub, and went right to bed. Mom knew that I was in trouble, passed by my bedroom, and paused several times. But each day I fared a little better.

My classmate and the other white college boys were walking across the yard with pads and pencils, doing inventories and similar tasks. Mr. Conley, a tough Irishman and my Dad's friend and boss for over twenty-five years, tried to get me such a job. When he couldn't, he asked me if I could type. He had me type in his office just off a work area. And although I had had a typing course, I couldn't type at the level he needed. So he assigned me to a labor group helping the bricklayers, doing real support work rather than either the most dirty work or often meaning-less work—cutting weeds around the railroad tracks or picking up litter in the courtyard.

The two bricklayers were white guys, Tom and Jim,

about thirty-five years old. Their regular bricklayer helper
was a black guy, Dennis, from Gary by way of Arkansas. I
was assigned while they were replacing the bricks of several down furnaces. And although the furnaces weren't
being used, they were still hot; they took days to cool. To
remove the used bricks we had to toss them to each other.
The bricks were so hot they usually wore a hole in my
gloves in one day.

I got to be good friends with Dennis. He was a hard
worker and great fun. He had tremendous eye-hand coordination and quickness. He used to entertain us by taking
a closed pocketknife—not a switchblade—from his pocket,
raise and open it in the blink of an eye. But he was also
often absent the day after payday; he was happy-go-lucky,
not serious.

Tom and Jim took me, a pre-college boy, seriously. They
sometimes talked to me about racial issues. A couple times
when we were talking about race, they'd say, "Take Dennis, for example. He takes the day off after payday. He
doesn't try to get ahead."

I asked them if they were members of the bricklayers
union.

"Of course," was the reply.

"Could Dennis become a member of the bricklayers
union?"

"Of course . . . well, now that you mention it, I don't
know."

I asked them whether they thought they would come to
work every day and do the best job they possibly could if
they knew that no matter how hard they worked they
could not move up from bricklayer helper to bricklayer.
They weren't turned off by my question. In fact, almost
every day after that they asked me what I thought about
black and white issues.

As Hugh Comer's son, I was everybody's safety project,
particularly Mr. Parker. He was a tall, dignified black man
who had known my father for many years and had been a

customer in the jewelry store where I had previously worked. One day we were working on a platform high above a closed-down but still smoldering furnace. The center of the platform was solid, but the boards were not nailed down. If you moved too far to the edge, the board would flip up and hurl you to certain death below. Mr. Parker told me to stick close to him, but my mind was drifting. I stepped too far to the edge and the board tilted. Mr. Parker grabbed my arm in a vicelike grip and pulled me to safety. I looked down at that still smoldering iron slag in the furnace below, and I almost died anyway— from fright and embarrassment. But nobody else on the platform saw it, and Mr. Parker put his finger over his lips, indicating that I should not say anything about it.

I learned a lot about the real world that summer. One payday I received my check and was walking home with Bill Robeson, a black college student. A car with an Illinois license plate pulled up. A man leaned out of the window and said, "Hey, little brother, come here, I want to ask you a question." I started toward the car, and Bill said, "Keep walking." The man rolled up the window and drove away. Bill explained to me that it was known that many of the men cashed their checks just outside the mill, drawing con artists, pickpockets, and thieves. That guy wanted to get me close to the car and grab my check.

One day I was dressing in the locker room when a fellow worker called me off to the side. "Look, sonny, how about loaning me five dollars until next payday?" It was the day after payday, and he was out of money already, having lost it in a crap game. He was a great big tough-looking dude. He wasn't going to intimidate me in that setting, but the specter of a grown man asking a young kid for five dollars the day after he was paid disturbed me.

Something was wrong in general, smoldering just below the surface, but you wouldn't have known it just by passing through our locker room. The locker rooms were assigned according to job areas. And since many blacks worked in low-level laboring jobs, most in my locker area were black. There was a great deal of warm banter, joke telling, kidding, loud laughter, and clowning. Some went out of their way to amuse the few whites in the room, but I didn't. My father had always said, "Never clown for the white man." But I was a good listener, and I enjoyed the jocularity, although it occurred to me that these men had nothing to be jocular about. My next thought was, "Perhaps that's just why they're so jocular."

One day a young man from Gary whose locker was next door to mine—one of the same guys who went out of his way to do his black stereotypes in front of the whites—was furious. There had been a race riot on the sand dunes the day before. The police and state troopers had turned out in force, and another confrontation was expected that evening. He invited me to come along "and kick some white ass." I declined. I didn't see him anymore that summer. Later, I was told that his leg had been broken by a policeman's billyclub.

Yes, I grew up a lot in the steel mill that summer.

College Days

"College days swiftly pass, imbued with memories fond." So goes a line from my fraternity hymn. My leaving home in September 1952 was a big production number, "Jimmy Goes to College." Dad stayed home into the fall in order to see a part of his dream come true. We all went down to Indiana University together in one car. We stopped and had a picnic lunch in a little town in central Indiana, Crawfordsville. I didn't see any black people around. (The town had no significance to me at the time, but it would.) The family got me settled on campus and returned home. I was euphoric, and scared.

I spent the first full day at college doing the usual registration things. At the end of the day I went for a snack at a sweetshop a half block off campus. I sat down at the counter and took a look at the menu. When I looked up, the owner was standing over me with his arm pointed toward the door, meaning "out." They didn't serve blacks. I was stunned. It took me a few seconds to comprehend. And then the anger seemed to move up from my legs through my body and threatened to explode in my head. I looked around for help. Nobody said anything. The man next to me looked straight ahead, motionless, silent. Totally humiliated and furious, I somehow moved through the door and stood on the sidewalk in front, looking back inside. I was helpless, devastated. I wanted to pick up a rock and smash the window of that sweetshop. I stumbled back to the dormitory and, in the quiet of my room, I cried. Welcome to Indiana University.

Two days later I went to a university orientation session. It began to rain cats and dogs, as only possible in southern Indiana. After the meeting administrators and professors pulled up in their cars to take as many students home as possible. Two or three cars filled to the gills. The fourth car pulled up. Two white students got in. I went in third. After that, nobody else wanted a ride. The driver tried to encourage my other classmates to get in, but they preferred to stand in the rain. The car was now polluted. As the professor drove towards the dormitories he tried to explain, "Maybe they didn't understand." But the explanation didn't work. He knew. After the where-are-you-from questions an awkward silence descended on the car. My euphoria of going to college was draining away.

I was not ready for it. I had been a BMHS (big man in high school). Dad had always said, "Work hard and achieve, and you will make it." I had assumed that he meant, be accepted. I had not really come to grips with what it meant to be black and from a low-income background. High-level achievers were a dime a dozen at the university. That crutch was not going to work. What *did* it mean to be black and low-income?

My notion of what college was about had been founded, in part, on movies—people dancing on tables, football heroics, sorority and fraternity frolics. But when I walked to class and crossed fraternity row on Jordan Street, I saw a great big invisible neon sign on all of the fraternities and sororities that read, "No blacks allowed." Affluent students cruised the campus in cars. I had five dollars a month as spending money.

My black roommate didn't survive the first two weeks and returned to New York City. A white student tried to become my roommate so that he would be close to a friend of his across the hall. He got the bureaucratic runaround—

"still occupied," "reallocating," "plans to use the room differently," and so on. He couldn't figure out what was going on. I could. The university did not assign blacks and whites to the same room.

The situation in the classroom was no better. I didn't work the first semester to make certain that I got off to a good start academically. But it didn't help. I was reeling with confusion and fear by the end of the first month. I had a flamboyant chemistry professor who picked out the same several students, turned on them quickly in the middle of the lecture, and asked a question. I was one of his selectees. I was also the only black student in a class of 350. The burden of proving black intelligence rested on my very slim shoulders. I would freeze, unable to respond even when I knew the answer. But often I didn't know it; I simply was not functioning well.

I did a lot of talking to myself that first semester. My head was in a constant swirl. Who am I? What's happening to me? Am I going to make it? I sometimes thought I was losing my mind. When it was all too much, I retreated to the movie house at the corner of the campus, a half block down the street from The Gables where Hoagy Carmichael wrote "Stardust." I would sit in the dark alone and escape into the film story.

I became a pledge to one of the three black fraternities on the campus, Alpha Phi Alpha, during the first semester. The fraternity served the purpose for which it was created, to give black students a sense of belonging and a place to express themselves on a predominantly white campus. We didn't have a fraternity house, but our chapter had some of the top students on campus. They had ranked first in academic achievement among *all* fraternities for the two previous years. The message was, "Oh yes we can." More important, the "brothers" advised us about the courses to take, about whom to avoid because of their racial attitudes, and provided other good advice. One of my frat brothers, Frank Hayes, had earned a Phi Beta Kappa key for academic excellence.

Frank, a friend of mine from high school, advised me not to take English Composition under Professor Sumner because he had never given a black student more than a C. I was still not convinced that a professor would judge a student on racial grounds. My approach had always been to find a way to make them honest.

The professor spoke like an Englishman, although he was an American. He played the part of Continental sophisticate—mentioning Josephine Baker, American jazz, and the like. He graded our compositions anonymously. One day he was reading my composition as an example of an A theme, praising the flow, the length of sentences, and so on. About midway he had a question and asked whose paper it was. I raised my black hand and like magic the quality of the paper went from A to F. He ripped it to shreds from that point on. I received a C for the course. From Sumner's standpoint, blacks could sing, dance, and play jazz music, but what could they *possibly* know about English composition?

I was the only black student in the composition class. Early the next semester, while walking across campus, I met a student from the course. When I told him that I had gotten a C, he couldn't believe it. He tried to offer an explanation, but finally dropped his head and mumbled, "That's not fair."

A number of white students understood what was going on and didn't approve, but couldn't do any more about it than the blacks. That year Crispus Attucks, the all-black high school in Indianapolis, won the state championship in basketball for the first time. But the referees made so many questionable calls that a white student who had graduated from the opposing high school got up and left the television room, saying, "If they're going to take it away, I don't want it."

I survived the first year, when many premeds decided to

opt out. Some black students played cards most of the first semester, flunked out, packed up, and went home. This was strange to me at the time, but as a psychiatrist I now understand it as rejection-avoidance behavior.

Some of my black friends considered me antisocial or biggety because I wouldn't play cards at lunch and in the evening, late into study time. I took a nap after dinner, got up, and hit the books. One friend of mine angrily told me that I thought I was better than him because he had gone to an all-black high school. I was very much hurt by that comment because it wasn't true. My feeling had always been that I would have had fewer problems at an all-black school. Late in the year another black student who wasn't doing well accused me of being a big shot, and started toward me in anger. He was bigger, but I fended him off until my black roommate from East Chicago, Ralph Hutchinson, grabbed and held him so that I could punch him. I just stood there. I couldn't hit him. But I realized I was catching it from both sides.

It was a time of cautious movement towards social integration. Race relations in the dormitory, unlike on the large campus, were generally fine. It was as if there were two states of being: Negroes as a group—not good; Negroes you knew as individuals—okay. Among blacks it was us and them. More and more I was relying on my black friends and organizations for my sense of well-being.

There was a black graduate student from Atlanta in my freshman dormitory complex. A few black undergrads and graduate students would discuss things, often the racial problem in the South. We Northerners were convinced that we lived in a more civilized and responsible culture. She defended Atlanta—not segregation—with tears in her eyes. Coming from the black Southern middle class, she knew black bankers, college presidents, businessmen. She belonged to a powerful black church; she had been a debutante. She was a part of the rich Southern black culture that we couldn't begin to understand. Because it was segregated, we automatically condemned it. It was only years later, when I fully understood the self and group affirmation role of black culture, that I began to understand what she was talking about.

I went home in June and recharged my self-esteem and confidence batteries. I visited people who cared about me— people from the church, schoolteachers, places I worked, and so on. I couldn't let my family and friends down, or let myself down.

On the weekends I often went to the Turf, a local bar and grill, where all of the college boys gathered. Occasionally guys I went to high school with who were now working in the steel mill would promise me that they would see me down at Indiana University next fall. "Okay, man, look me up," I would say. But he knew and I knew that he wouldn't be there. And when I was old enough to drink, I didn't have to buy. It was a matter of honor and status for the guys in the mill—they paid.

Madison Turner, my childhood friend, came by to see me just before I went back to campus. We had talked briefly over the fence earlier in the summer. But this time, after a few remembrances, there was an awkward silence. We had been growing apart for years, and now we had little in common. As he left, we looked at each other on opposite sides of the screen door. There was sadness in his eyes. It was like two people standing on the rear platform of the caboose of separate trains on the same track, but moving in opposite directions. I ached inside.

Love and Hate

Having recharged my batteries in East Chicago, I returned to Bloomington ready to roll. Dropping my extracurricular activities and not working the first semester of my freshman year had been a mistake. During the second year I worked as a cafeteria busboy, made top academic honors, and was very active in the fraternity. That year I was the vice-president.

When I got home the summer of 1954, things were really looking up. Dad had bought a brand-new Chevrolet to be shared among the four of us. He had bought some land and built a house for his parents in Alabama many years before. Like many black Southerners, he had planned to make some money, return South, and build his own home, but never did. When a niece offered to buy a parcel of the land, he sold it. Since it was not enough money to pay for our entire college education, he reasoned that it would be better used to give us a "glimpse of the good life." We didn't need the motivation, but we were delighted to have a car.

I returned to school my junior year in grand style—good sophomore grades, president of the fraternity, and a new car. Who could ask for anything more? And yet, more was right around the corner.

The first week back I was driving down the street with a friend when we passed two black coeds. They were both attractive, but one caught my attention in particular—slender, even skinny, with chiseled facial features and big, beautiful eyes. "Who is that!" I asked.

The next night I met her at our fraternity dance. We danced. We talked. She was from Crawfordsville, Indiana, the same town we had stopped in on my way to college the first time. "Of course there are other blacks in town," she said in response to my inquiry, "about a hundred. My father is the president of the local NAACP." Her name was Shirley Arnold.

We made plans to go to a roller skating party the next day. I was so nervous about the date that I procrastinated. A half an hour late, I met her and her friends—having given up on me coming—walking toward the rink. I couldn't skate; she was very good.

We had a third date and this time I was on time. I was a fancy dancer, "a showoff," she said, but it was okay. She was not pretentious or phony. She thought I was down to earth. I thought she was something special.

At a picnic for two that summer, by a little stream in Indianapolis—she had on a beautiful white dress with large red circles—I began to feel very special about her.

But while that first date with Shirley turned out better than I could have imagined, that semester did not live up to its early promise. First of all, I worried a lot about Dad. My heart sank whenever I received a long-distance telephone call: it might be the bad news.

I made two A's a B and an F, in physics, that semester. I was plain self-destructive. For some reason I stopped studying physics. I knew that it was another of the big premedical hurdles, but I just could not say, "You can."

It was during this very difficult period that I tried to hate all white people. Dad's condition was not improving, and hadn't it been the white system that had caused his illness? My dream of becoming a doctor was being threatened. School integration and other racial disturbances in the South were making headlines. Wasn't it white folks who were giving me—us—hell?

About midway through the physics course one of the women students asked me if I would like to study with her. She was white. Every warning I had ever received leaped into my head, but I agreed. It was an unmitigated disaster. We studied in the lounge area, in front of full-length windows next to a long walkway. People of every age gawked, did a double take, bumped into each other taking a look at us. I couldn't concentrate at all.

Shortly after that my roommate, Donald Perry, was coming down the hill near our dormitory at dusk. He looked more like a happy-go-lucky Ichabod Crane than a "black, brute, rapist." But a white female student looked up and saw him coming down the path and ran away screaming. He was left standing there, saying, "Come back, little girl, I'm not going to bother you." He hadn't done anything. The stereotype was in her mind. Shortly afterward, two black students from the floor below stuck Ku Klux Klan signs under our door. We laughed about it, but it was laughter to keep from crying.

I took my medical-school interview during that semester because there was a program of admission after three years at Indiana. It was rumored that no more than two blacks a year were admitted to the medical school. With a good junior-year performance I could be accepted, but there were four black seniors and several black foreign students being interviewed. I imagined that they would have first preference for "our" quota. The interview was an intimidating experience. It was in a huge room. The ornate furniture, huge chandeliers, the cold, distant style of the interviewers was foreign to my class and culture. I was not admitted.

But even so, I was tempermentally and cognitively un-suited to be a hater. Once, while I was struggling with my frustrations and feelings, I was talking to a friend at the bottom of a stairwell. A white coed was talking to a friend at the top. She turned and started down the stairs, lost her balance, and hurtled down the stairs two, three at a time, trying to regain her balance. She was going to hit a concrete wall. I was so angry with white people that for an instant I didn't move. But I couldn't do that. I moved over and blocked her fall. And I felt guilty and mixed up because she was so appreciative.

Because Dad was ill at home, because I was embarrassed about physics, confused about many things—and I could save money—I decided to take the second semester of my junior year at the Indiana University Extension in East Chicago. When I arrived at midyear, one of the neighbors commented, "I knew that old boy wasn't going to make it." It was the same lady who suggested that Mom have me gargle with urine for a sore throat and who had suggested that she name me Depression, because I was born during the Depression. I'm sure glad Mom ignored her.

Dad was perplexed by my grades—two A's a B, and an F. It was the first time I ever heard him suggest that a problem might be racial. Mom suspected something more complicated. While I was looking out the living room window, trying to figure out what the hell was going on, she came up behind me. She pointed out that my grades were very uneven. She wondered why I couldn't do as well as the Hayes boys were doing. They were black friends from home, sons of a physician, both Phi Beta Kappas. I knew not to suggest to Mom that maybe I wasn't able to do as well. I didn't have an answer. In fact, I was so hurt, confused, and scared I couldn't say a word. She sensed that the problem was more than my not working hard enough. Finally she made the statement that took the monkey off my back: "Well, do the best you can, but don't ruin your health. You are more important to us than your being a doctor or anything else."

You know, from the day I hadn't been able to play the piano for Mrs. Boyd's guests, a part of me had wondered whether my achievement was more important than my being in my mom's eyes. I found out. I was relieved, and ready to struggle again.

When I returned to the campus in my senior year, I had a steady girlfriend, a car, and I was a leader in my fraternity. I wore white bucks and yellow corduroy pants, the mid-1950s trademark of seniors. I made A's in all but one two-hour course. I applied and was admitted to several medical schools early in the year.

Confident in myself, I began challenging the racism I saw all around me. Early that fall, our dormitory invited several sororities, one black, to a dance as part of a program to create good relationships between "the Greeks" and the "non-Greeks." After a couple white guys expressed disapproval, they disinvited the black sorority. I presented the case before the student judicial body, and we received strong student and faculty support. The sorority was reinvited.

In the spring of that year the baseball team had planned to leave its black catcher at home because of segregation in the South. I wrote a letter of objection to the student newspaper. Professors and students, black and white, stopped me on campus to support my position. Because of the pressure generated, the catcher was included in the trip. On his return he jokingly thanked me for helping him learn how to eat from a bag outside of restaurants.

After I interviewed before the medical school admissions board at Indiana the second time, I thought that I had blown it. I was angry because despite my setback in physics, I had come out with a very strong third year; a white friend with a lesser record had been admitted. One of the interviewers asked me in a hostile voice, "Who is the attorney general of the United States?"—the kind of question asked to test the well-roundedness of medical school applicants. He looked like a white redneck. Anxious in the first place, I couldn't think of the Attorney General's name. Another interviewer noticed the tension between me and his colleague. In a mediating way he asked me to describe some of the attorney general's activities.

"He's investigating the Emmett Till case," I snapped. Emmett Till was a twelve-year-old black kid from Chicago who had been lynched that past summer, 1955, in Mississippi for eyeballing a white woman. To make matters worse, one of the members of the interviewing panel kept going through my record, and finally showed the folder to another colleague. "I don't know why this boy wasn't admitted last year," he said. His comment was ignored. I sat there stewing. I left the room emotionally drained.

I had been taught to keep my cool: "Never give them an excuse to turn you down." And yet, in the most important moment of my life, I had lost my cool.

Despite my display of anger, several months later I was admitted to the Indiana University School of Medicine. But so many difficult, confusing things had happened over those four years that I felt that I needed a black college experience.

Maggie's Job Corps

The summer before my junior year, 1954, had been the worst job market in many years. Mom pressed Continental Foundry to the point that they had me come out and look at a job, but warned that it was too dangerous. It was. Solidified iron fragments had to be dislodged from a bucket three times my height. Mom drew the line on obviously dangerous work. When I didn't have a job by the second week home, I was really depressed. Dad said to me as he left for Arizona, "Don't worry. Your mother will get you a job." And she did—as a stockboy in the A&P. It paid less, but it was better than nothing.

In the summer of 1955 the economic recession continued. The steel mills still weren't hiring. Norman had gotten into Youngstown Sheet and Tube the summer he finished high school, so he was hired again in 1955. I went out to see if I could get a job there. There was a long, long, long line of men of all ages and all races waiting to apply. I came back home and told Mom that it was impossible. She picked up the telephone and called the personnel office and went into her act:

"My son already works for you. He's Norman Comer, the football player and honor student who is at Northwestern University." She paused for effect. "Norman's brother, Jim, needs a job."

"Oh, yes, fine boy, Norman. But we're not hiring any

college students this year, Mrs. Comer. We made an exception for Norman."

"Yes, I know that and I appreciate that. But I have these four children all trying to go to school. Their father is sick and living in Arizona, and he can't support these children. I'm doing the best I can to hold this family together. And we're not asking for a handout, we want to work, my boys want to work."

"I know, Mrs. Comer, but we have a long line of men out here who have to support families and need to work, but we've got to turn them down."

"Yes, but my kids are trying to go to college. Now, you sound like a decent person. And you know that many of your people say that our people don't want to help themselves, don't want to work. I've got these four children who want to work, who want to go to college, who want to make something of themselves so that they can help our people. That will be for your benefit and for our benefit."

He paused for such a long time she called his name to make sure that he was still there. He finally said, "Okay, Mrs. Comer, send Jim back out here. But have him come around to the side door so that the other men won't see him come in ahead of them."

I had returned and filled out the application when another roadblock popped up. I have twenty-two hundred vision in one eye. I was flunking the eye test! The examiner looked in distress at the personnel officer who had talked to Mom on the telephone. I was desperately trying to think of a solution when the examiner dropped his pencil. In retrospect, I suspect that he received a nonverbal message to find a way; I didn't hear any conversation between him and the personnel officer. When he leaned down to pick up the pencil, I looked at the test for the bad eye with my good eye and memorized as much of the content as I could. When he started the exam again, I gave him the bad-eye material from memory. He said, "Good enough," and I was hired.

Once when I was a kid, the fruit truck—the same one I later worked on—came through the neighborhood and a basket of peaches fell off. All the kids around grabbed as many peaches as they could and ran. That was stealing in my opinion and I had been taught not to do so, but I wanted a peach. So I went home and asked Mom for a peach from the refrigerator. She refused and left me sitting out on the back porch, confused. A short while later she came out and gave me a peach and said, "But let that be a lesson to you. Sometimes you must get while the getting is good." Passing the eye test was one of those times. It is a fine line that still bothers me.

There was no receiving line at the Youngstown Sheet and Tube. Nobody knew my dad, and I went immediately to the tough jobs. In the heat of the summer, near machines rolling white-hot steel, I cleaned sludge out from the pit of a closed-down rolling machine. In boots almost up to my hips I waded in water almost three feet deep, with slippery footing. The pit contained water used to cool the steel, oil, and grease used in the operation. We had to shovel it out in buckets. I was always afraid I was going to lose my footing, fall, not be able to get up in those huge boots—and never be heard from again.

On another job I was part of a crew that had to spread sand in a train freight car as it was poured from a crane bucket above. Again we had boots and shovels. You had to move fast because the weight of the falling sand and the increasing accumulation made the area around you move like quicksand. So I tossed sand like crazy because, surrounded by macho men, I didn't want to have them stop for me.

One weekend we lined up for jobs, and the supervisor said that he needed two big men for a tough job. I was one of the smallest guys in the group; I knew he wouldn't call my number. He looked around the group and pointed to a black kid, a football player who had just finished high school and·was on his way to college. He looked around again and pointed at me. I was stunned, but then I understood. He didn't mean he had a tough job. He meant he had a nigger's job. There were only two black kids there that day, and, college kids or not, the blacks did the dirty and dangerous work. For two days I used an air hammer that weighed almost as much as I did to break concrete.

But as tough as some of the jobs were, I preferred them to the make-work jobs. There is nothing more boring than chopping weeds around the railroad tracks. For one two-week period I replaced the custodians when they went on vacation. The first day I finished an eight-hour assignment in a half an hour. The boss called me over to the side and said, "Look, sonny, you got to take your time. These are old men and they can't work so fast—got it?" I got it. But I also began to wonder why people who worked had no sympathy for people who didn't because they couldn't get jobs. What was the difference?

Again the mostly black locker room was a warm, "happy" place. Simmering resentment exploded one day during my second summer. The black men were absolutely furious. They had heard about Emmett Till's lynching. They'd talk about it a few minutes, and somebody would pick up something and throw it across the room. One banged his hand repeatedly on a locker. I ached in the pit of my stomach. The few white guys in that locker room dressed and got out of there as fast as they could.

Norman and I used to talk during our breaks and at lunchtime. Norm broke me up one day with a story about an adviser he had at Northwestern. His advisor was less than enthusiastic about his responsibility—"a dumb black jock, no counseling needed." But in going through the motions he almost disdainfully asked him about his hobbies. "Listening to classical music," Norm replied. He listened to classical music for hours. He read all about the musicians and the music.

The adviser almost fell out of his chair. By then Norm had picked up the implications of his response and began to lay it on him—listing his favorite compositions, when they were written, when first performed, under what conditions, and on and on. The adviser listened in stunned amazement and then asked questions trying to figure out who he was and why this interest. And the answer, a steel mill worker's son from East Chicago, Indiana, didn't provide a clue. We enjoyed blowing stereotypes out of the water.

Several times on summer weekends we went with a few buddies to the nightclubs on the South Side of Chicago—the Kitty Kat, the Persian Hotel—warm nights, cool jazz, fine, oh so fine women. The streets were not yet mean. We would stand on the corner talking, observing. One night my college roommate and I stood watching the prostitutes ply their trade. Limousines squiring men of all colors pulled up and talked deals. Several women came over and made us propositions. Finally a prostitute who had been watching us came over and made an offer. When we declined, she said, "Y'all boys go on home. Y'all don't want nuthin'."

One way or another, we got jobs, or Mom got us jobs, every summer during our college years. Without jobs or loans we would not have made it. One time when we were all but out of money, Charles had to take a summer practicum course in the optometry program. With nowhere to turn for the money, Mom called Indiana University and asked to speak to the president. Flabbergasted, the operator tried to explain to her that you couldn't just call and speak to the president. Mom insisted and eventually got the scholarship and loan office officer—and the needed money.

Dad's Death

In the spring of 1954 Mom began to help Dad pack up his things for the summer return to East Chicago. She put aside the things he would need when he returned to Phoenix. Dad said, "Take it all."

"But you're going to need these when you get back," Mom pointed out.

"I'm not coming back."

He had spent most of the past five years in Arizona, and he wasn't getting better. He sorely missed his family, missed seeing us grow into young adults. He probably knew that he didn't have much longer to live. In fact, the gift of the car was his last big effort to motivate us to achieve our goals.

That summer of my sophomore year was a good summer for him. Many of the church people came by to visit. He even went to a few church services. I was nineteen years old and Thelma, the youngest, was fifteen. Dad watched with pleasure the comings and goings—to parties, ball games, and work—of the little children he left and the young men and women he returned to. Our family dinners and debate had a special vitality that summer.

In the fall Norman went off to college as a freshman and I returned as a junior. Dad's wheezing and labored breathing was evident throughout the summer, but he was able to get about. Soon after we left he had to have oxygen therapy more often, and his condition began to decline. When I returned home at midyear, January 1955, he rallied for a while. He was up and about, and his condition appeared to improve with the spring weather. Despite his health I never really acknowledged the probability that he was going to die soon. I couldn't. The only sign that things had changed was a growing irritability. Once in the spring we were planting the flower garden together and I was fooling around with Chuck. Dad got so upset he raised his hand as if to cuff me. That was the first time he had ever done that, and I was twenty, not ten. He was immediately embarrassed when he caught himself. And I felt badly about making him that upset.

He talked to Mom about the jobs she was helping us get for the summer. They talked about plans for Charles attending college the next year and Thelma the year after. And then suddenly without warning, just after the Fourth of July, his condition turned critical. He was bedridden, on almost constant oxygen use, sweating profusely in the July heat and unair-conditioned bedroom, struggling for every breath. It was a painful sight. Yet he never complained.

In the last week his condition was so critical that one of us sat up with him at all times—me, Norman, the man upstairs, Mom. On the morning of July 20 I was helping Mom change Dad's bed. I had been waiting to hear about possible admission to medical school. Dad pulled me to him and asked me whether I had heard anything. I told him that I had not, but assured him that I would get in, that I would become a doctor. He was disappointed. He knew he was dying. He wanted to hear that I had been admitted before he died.

About an hour later my cousin Johnny Lee was passing and a neighbor told him that he'd better go in, that Dad was critical. Moments after that, Mom, John, and I were huddled around his bed, helping him move to the edge, when he looked up at us and said, "Oh, oh." His head dropped. He was gone.

I wasn't prepared for it. I rushed to the telephone and called Dr. Boyd. He told me that he couldn't come out right then. I couldn't believe it. I said, "You've got to come! You've got to save him!"

Dr. Boyd replied quietly, understandingly, "Jimmy, I'm sure your papa's gone. I've got an office full of sick people. I can't leave. I'll be out as soon as I can."

I was stunned. "Dad can't die. Not yet—not yet—I'm not in medical school yet!" I had fantasized as a ten- or eleven-year-old that I would become a doctor and cure him.

When Dr. Boyd arrived several hours later he knew that I was upset. He explained to me that Dad had been dying for several weeks and that everything that could be done had been done. He put his arms around me and said, "You were blessed to have had a great father. And now you'll have to carry on—finish school and live out his dreams. That's what he would want from you. You've got to pull yourself together and help your mother."

I had a painful lump in my throat and my eyes were brimming with tears, but I knew that he was right on all scores.

Mom was devastated. When Dr. Boyd walked in the house she threw her arms around his neck and cried. He had known us through so many good times—and now the bad times. Mom put a cot just inside the dining room, lay across it, and went into deep mourning. Mom and Dad had had a special kind of relationship, and we all knew it. Dad had been the first person who ever cared about her and cared for her. He gave her instructions in the ways of life and the ways of love. As she said many times, "He was a father, a teacher, a husband, and a saviour." So deep was her silent despair that I worried about her.

Football practice at Northwestern had started that week, but Norman hadn't wanted to go because of Dad's critical condition. Mom and Dad had encouraged him to go. I met him when he got out of the car and told him that Dad had died and how Mom was taking it. Thelma and Charles came home from summer school, and Louise came home from work. We all decided that we were going to help Mom by keeping a stiff upper lip.

Despite Mom's deep mourning she gave instructions for the funeral. I was sent to town to make the floral arrangements. I parked downtown and all along the way I met people who had heard that Dad had passed, and they expressed their sympathy. As I crossed the park I met Katy Mason, a sister from our church. She said, "I am so sorry to hear that your father passed. He was a fine man. They just don't make men like your father anymore." She went on and on. Finally she said, "I hope you'll grow up to be a great man just like your father. We need more men like him." She stopped, looked at me, and said, "Aw, you ain't going to be like your father! Young folks today just ain't made of the same stuff." She stalked away, as if irritated by the fact that there was no replacement for Dad. As hurt as I was by Dad's death, I was mildly amused by her charge, and also challenged.

The funeral was on a Monday, a bad day for a funeral in a steel mill town. Everybody is at work. But it had to be held that day in order to give his sisters in Alabama time to travel to East Chicago. Nonetheless, the church was packed to overflowing. Many men had taken a day off, most without pay. The top executives from the steel mill were there, leading officials in town, lots of church people, and most of our young friends.

The way one is put away was, and still is, a measure of one's stature in the black community. Dad was put away nice. There was a handsome slate-gray casket, many floral offerings, and an overflow crowd. Aunt Mada and Aunt Rosie were distraught. Aunt Mada kept crying, "Come home, Hugh," which had been the family's desire since he was a young man. Many people in the South still had the notion that the North was bad for their people, that they could come home and be saved, not gobbled up by steel mills and the like. Mrs. Butler sang one of Dad's favorite songs: "Life is like a mountain railroad/With an engineer that's brave/We must make the run successful/From the cradle to the grave."

Norman, Chuck, and I were among the pallbearers, but Mom was so distraught that I joined with others in helping her from the church. As she came out of the door she was surprised and pleased to see so many people packed around the stairs and out into the street. And as we went down Euclid Avenue for the traditional last ride through town, as far as you could see there were cars in the funeral procession. It helped the pain, if only for a little while.

During this period we all slipped away to our private mourning places, out of Mom's sight. I usually went to the basement. During one of those visits I found a box with a collection of Dad's papers. Among the papers I found Dad's reflections on the life and loss to the community of Mr. Turner, a fellow deacon and friend, written at the time of his death years before. The book was not a daily diary, but a record of major events that had taken place in our church and community. I was surprised to realize that this tough steel mill worker had also been a thoughtful writer.

One of Mom's friends advised her to keep Norman out of school because he was the biggest and had the best chance of surviving in the steel mills. I was the oldest and felt that I had some responsibility to help support the family. Some people told Mom that it made no sense to think of sending all of us to school in the first place. Norman considered dropping out of school because I was one year away from finishing. I would be Mom's first birth child to finish college. He felt that he already had one year and could come back and finish later. And if not, at least one of us would have graduated. Mom was not having any of it. She insisted that both of us return to school, and

Chuck was sent off to school for the first time that fall. "We'll go as far as the money takes us and then see what happens."

After Dad's death Mom tried to get a job everywhere. She had no formal education and could barely read and write. The personnel officer at the steel mill where Dad had worked told her that because he had not wanted her to work in the mill while he was living, they didn't feel that it would be right to hire her now that he was gone. But I suspect that the continued economic recession had a lot to do with that decision. The personnel officer at St. Catherine's Hospital wanted very much to help her, and us, but didn't want her to work in housekeeping, the only job for which she had skills. He asked her for suggestions. She noted that the elevator had only part-time, after-school workers and suggested that they could use a full-time person. She ran the elevator for the next six years, retiring after my internship.

Three months after Dad's death the entire family went to Evanston for the Indiana–Northwestern football game. Mom was in seventh heaven that day. Norman was the first-string fullback for Northwestern. We were all awed by the affluence and pomp—limousines, well-heeled old grads, tailgating before the game, and meeting the ball-players after. It took us into another world.

I solved my loyalty dilemma by cheering for Norm when he carried the ball and for Indiana otherwise. In the fourth quarter Norm made a touchdown-saving tackle on the Olympic decathalon hero, Milt Campbell. To this day Mom remembers that Norman stopped Milt Campbell. Indiana won, but that didn't matter. We could feel that we were in striking distance of making it. It was a day Dad would have cherished.

Two years after Dad passed, Mom married Mr. Robin-son, a deacon in a church in another section of town. We were all out of the house by that time, and so he was more a friend than a stepfather. He had his own young adult family to provide for, although they lived separately. He was not responsible for, nor did he contribute to, our education at all. But the respect and friendship was mutual. He and Mom were married for twenty-five years until his death in 1984.

Medical School

Being black in America is often like playing your home games on the opponents' court. Instead of cheers you get jeers—and worse. By the time I was a senior in college, I felt good about Indiana University. I had overcome, and a number of people had helped me. But I was tired. Why did I have to fight? I just wanted to be a student, not a black student who had to prove something every step of the way. I wanted to feel that the school was my place—home court. For this reason I elected to go to the predominantly black Howard University College of Medicine in Washington, D.C., rather than to Indiana University.

In 1956 the nation's capitol had only recently desegregated downtown stores, movie houses, and other facilities. I could not believe the rundown housing conditions only a few blocks from the White House. On the taxi ride from the railroad station to my dormitory room at Carver Hall, I saw children playing in squalor. Adult men sat on doorsteps, apparently without work. Everywhere buildings were abandoned or stood in advanced stages of deterioration.

Even then the two black worlds that are nowadays more visible existed, but the gap was less apparent. The walk from the medical school to Carver Hall was through a heavily populated housing project. Barefoot children stood in open doors. Some begged us for money. The Washing-

178

ton Senators were still playing baseball in Griffith Stadium right next to the medical school, and the more entrepreneurial kids "protected" the cars of fans for a small fee.

On the other hand, Carver Hall was a future "Who's Who in Black America." Vernon Jordan, former president of the National Urban League, lived on the first floor. Doug Wilder, the first black lieutenant governor of Virginia, and his roommate Henry Marsh, the first black mayor of Richmond, lived across the hall from me on the second floor. Andrew Young's brother, then a dental student, also lived at Carver. One of my classmates left medicine for law after the first year and became one of the country's most successful black businessmen. The place was crammed full of future doctors, lawyers, and leaders who would make a name for themselves across the country in years to come.

One of my classmates' uncle was dean of the chapel. He had us out to dinner early in the semester. He was one of the most brilliant people I've ever met. I visited the home of a surgeon who was one of the early black graduates of Indiana University Medical School. He lived on the northwest Black Gold Coast with row after row of black middle and upper income homes—large, beautiful structures with well-kept lawns. I had never seen a black neighborhood like that. It was like the Park Addition in my hometown, where only white people lived.

During the first week I was swept up in the whirl of "the hill"—the home of the undergraduates. I could not believe it. It was like being in a candy store with every color of chocolate from white to dark. I had never met so many attractive black women at one time in all my life. I got lost trying to find the infirmary and asked a coed for directions. She was so beautiful I lost my concentration. I thanked her and a block away I had to ask somebody else.

Many of my classmates were also refugees from predominantly white schools, and most of them had elected to go to Howard for the same reasons that I had. Some were from small black schools that I had never heard of, but most were from the best-known black schools—Howard, Lincoln, Morehouse. One black student who was from Tougaloo, a small black college in Mississippi, did average work for the first year and then became a top student in the class in the second. He told me that he was intimidated by the competition from big-name schools. Being among so many attractive, intelligent, affluent, high-achieving blacks was just what the doctor ordered for me. But again I had to struggle. And in the struggle I came to realize that not all the problems in life are black and white.

I arrived on campus with a middle-ear infection. I also had a then undiagnosed allergy to fall pollen. My eyes were red, my ears were plugged and aching, and I felt like my head was in a fishbowl. During orientation I heard one of the deans tell us that one out of three students wouldn't make it. I looked to my left and to my right, and both people looked smarter than me. Suddenly I was scared. I flunked the first round of quizzes in almost everything. To make matters worse, I was allergic to the formaldehyde used to preserve the cadavers in anatomy. I had a hacking dry cough the entire first year.

Also, there were cliques at Howard, just as at Indiana—middle income, low income; light skinned, dark skinned; "good" (white) hair, "bad" hair; Northeastern, Midwestern, Southern, and West Indian. I was a low-income, in-between skin, "bad" hair kid from the Midwest—not a winner. Even so, the sense of belonging seemed to be based more on ability than on membership in these particular groups.

I had come too far to lose out now. I heard my mother's admonition: "You can learn just as well as anybody else . . . and you'd better!" September turned to October and hayfever season was over. I rallied. By the second round of exams I was doing average work, and by the third I was doing very well.

At Howard I discovered that I did not want to be a leader. I did not have to lead; there were plenty of good leaders in my class. I gradually became aware of the bind I had been in on the predominantly white Indiana campus. I had been trying to carry the race. I had tried to disprove the myths and stereotypes—blacks are poor in math, they are overly emotional, they are inarticulate. Too much of my motivation for learning had been negative: "I'll show them."

At Howard I was free from all this. I had been playing the role of acceptable Negro. I began to relax and swing with a group of fellows who were comfortable being black. Class parties were like none I had ever been to before. There was a real sense of belonging. I met many teachers who had a special dedication to black education and a sensitivity born of shared experience.

Sometimes, though, I found just the opposite. Some of the professors were bright, aggressive people who had never achieved the recognition they were due because they were black. Their choice of employment had been limited; professional societies had barred them; professional organizations had failed to recognize important work. Perhaps as a result, the spark had gone out of several once dynamic teachers. Their frustration was taken out on the students.

On one occasion I lost twenty-five points on an exam because I didn't use the problem-solving formula the professor claimed he discovered. All of the calculations that gained me the correct answer were on the paper. When I showed him he said angrily, "When you get a laboratory and a National Institute of Health research grant you can use your formula. Until then, you use mine."

One professor teased us about having it so easy, being on scholarships and loans. When he had been in medical school he had had a full-time job and sent half of his earnings home to support his impoverished family in Baltimore. Many of my professors had worked, often full-time, while going to school. When I was growing up, I had read that Abraham Lincoln walked miles to school each day—an example of the will to succeed among the "builders of our nation"—while I was taught in many subtle and not-so-subtle ways that black people were too lazy to expend any energy to improve themselves.

The summer before medical school, I had worked as an orderly at St. Catherine's Hospital in my hometown. Because I was planning to become a general practitioner in East Chicago, I felt that I should get to know people and patients at the hospital. I had been told that I could not serve as an extern (similar to an intern) until after my first two years of medical school. But early in the summer after my first year, Dr. Steen, the director of training, overheard me telling a former high school classmate that I was a medical student, and immediately accepted me into the externship program. I learned a great deal as an orderly—medicine from the bedpans up.

For example, there was an extern who was very bright but very arrogant. He chewed out nurses twice his age and with ten times more experience. Finally they decided to let him hang himself. He made a treatment error on a patient that a couple of nurses knew about, but wouldn't tell him. The extern's pride was wounded; the patient paid with pain and suffering. I vowed that when I became a doctor I would treat all my coworkers—professionals and nonprofessionals—with respect.

The notion was probably easier for me to hold than some. One of my nonprofessional coworkers was the lady on the elevator—Mom. She told everybody about her son, "the doctor." Some who didn't know us thought the elevator lady must surely be kidding. She had a great rapport and great respect for most of the doctors, but she saw some things she didn't like and made it clear that she didn't want that behavior from me. "When you get to be a doctor, I don't want you talking about 'the heart case' in room 202. That's a person with a name, family, and friends."

I began clinical clerkships in my third year, and I enjoyed all of them except psychiatry. I began to think about specializing in each one—surgery, obstetrics and gynecology, internal medicine, dermatology, opthamalogy—all except psychiatry. I was amused by the theories. I laughed during the clinical lectures and joked that it was witch doctoring. I was assigned to a catatonic schizophrenic patient for four weeks. She didn't speak to me the entire time, *maybe* a faint smile when I said good-bye. And the next summer while an extern at St. Catherine's a patient developed acute paranoid symptoms and threatened me and his doctor, temporarily trapping us in his room. I knew that this specialty was not for me.

Late in my junior year I began to struggle with the question of whether I wanted to be a general practitioner or a specialist, even whether I wanted to be a doctor or not. True, I was Hugh and Maggie's son, the doctor. But I was a people person, a social-problem person, and medical training seemed to be carrying me further away from my interests than toward them. These doubts would not solidify, though, until later.

My senior year, one of the most rewarding I have ever had, was marred only by one incident. During my pediatric clerkship I worked with an intern trying to save an infant who had been burned by hot water knocked off the stove in her congested apartment. Several times it looked like the baby was going to make it. Then she died. I was devastated and I thought the mother would be. I dreaded facing her. But when she heard, she stoically said, "Well, it was God's will." I wanted to scream out that God had nothing to do with it, that the conditions they lived under were man-made. But I looked at the peace and comfort that her faith gave her—and remembered that I was a medical student—and held my tongue.

Mom and Mr. Robinson came down for graduation. It was a glorious graduation day. When I stood to take the Hippocratic Oath, I was in another world. It was the culmination of my greatest hope, my highest aspiration; all thereafter would be icing on the cake. As I took my seat, even though he couldn't be there, I could see Dad beaming with pride.

Norman finished college in 1958, Thelma and Charles in 1959. We would all obtain additional graduate degrees later on, but the major hurdle was over. Mom's dream, Dad's dream, our dream had come true.

PART III

ALL OUR CHILDREN

Intern

Shirley and I had been married the summer before, on June 20, 1959, in a Methodist church in Crawfordsville, Indiana. Mom, Mr. Robinson, all my brothers and sisters, her family, and, I believe, all the one hundred black people and some of the whites in Crawfordsville were there. We had absolutely no money so that after the wedding night in Indianapolis, we spent a day in Chicago and the rest of our "honeymoon" with Shirley's Aunt Bess and Uncle Les in Milwaukee.

We had planned not to have children for several years, but sensible is something you are *before* your wedding. We were married in June, school started in September, and she learned she was expecting in October. She was, however, able to work right up until school was out in June.

About three weeks after I started my internship at St. Catherine's Hospital our son, Brian, was born. We lived in an apartment at the hospital, and when Shirley went into labor, one of the nuns was to bring the stretcher around. When we got to the stairs it looked like all the nuns in the hospital were there. I had worked there for four previous summers and Shirley had worked there the summer before, and so there was a lot of interest in the new baby. Dr. Boyd, the same doctor who had delivered me, delivered Brian. And so my internship began on a terrific personal upbeat.

Several weeks after Brian's birth, Shirley went to work as a nurse in the hospital on the 3–11 shift and, with the help of my cousin Ruth, I took care of him. Sometimes I would get evening emergency calls and would take him on the ward with me; the nurses would care for him while I took care of the patients. On one occasion I was called to the ward to treat a woman who had gone into insulin shock. I recognized her son. It was the same kindergarten classmate who had taken me by his house to show his mother that a black kid had given a party in school. Recovery from insulin shock is quick and dramatic, and she came to as we stood there. When her son told her that we had been classmates she said, "So many of you kids have done so well." Obviously she had forgotten that she had once, in effect, expected a life of drunken brawls for me. But I remembered, and I felt a surge of vindication; I had shown her.

Toward the end of my internship, Dr. Ramker, a general practitioner with a huge practice, asked me if I would like to join a group that was going to build a clinic in a booming suburban area. The group was all white. They were also fine physicians, so I was honored to be asked. I knew that they were going to do extremely well financially, and they did. But one of the reasons I had always wanted to become a doctor was not only to provide medical care, but to improve conditions in the black community. I knew that I could not do that in the suburbs. I expressed my appreciation and declined.

At the same time, my moonlighting experiences were forcing me to rethink my general-practice plans. There were five black doctors and a black surgeon in East Chicago—Dr. Boyd being one of them. I had a special relationship with all of them and I was very close to one in particular, Dr. Bryant. In fact, I was considering going into practice with him. For this reason—and because I needed the money—I did some moonlighting for him toward the end of my internship. I worked a few evenings and off days in his office to get a feel for things. It was a way for me to look at his practice and for him to look at me.

He had one of the largest practices in town, mostly black and poor. The office was located above the drugstore across the street from the Turf, the same bar and grill where I had enjoyed hanging out as a college student. Some of the people from that period were still hanging out on the same corner. "Hey, Doc" "Look at my man with his doctor bag" "Give me a shot, Doc" was the banter as I walked through the area.

Ed and I treated more than fifty patients a day. Penicillin here, B-12 there, an abcess, a laceration, high blood pressure—the gamut. What I kept noticing, though, was that a large number of people were simply depressed. Many had physical complaints without any obvious cause. Ed had a way with words and could pump them up so that they could go back and manage the world for a couple weeks, but I wasn't sure I could do that. It wasn't my style. Why are so many people in despair? I kept asking myself.

Ed was called home on family business, and I took over his practice for a week. The first day I saw more than fifty patients by myself. I went on a house call in a very poor neighborhood to treat a young child for an infection. When I was done, the grandmother asked me my fee. I looked around at the poverty-strickened conditions of the home and I stammered and stuttered. She looked at me and said, "Son, you better learn to charge or you going to starve out here." I took the money, but I didn't feel good about it.

That week, it was one thing after another. I was called to Block Avenue, a dangerous street, in the middle of the night. It turned out that the patient was a young drug addict who claimed she was sick when she was not—disturbing my sleep without cause—in order to keep her sister from throwing her out of the house. Another patient fainted in the office, became cold and clammy, and we called the ambulance to take her to the hospital. When I got there she had fully recovered; I later learned that it was a trick she pulled on every new doctor in town. When I was home I couldn't relax because I was waiting for the telephone to ring—for what might or might not be a legitimate need. Again, I wanted to be a doctor, in part, to use my power to address social problems. The way it was going, I wasn't going to have time to even think about social problems, not to mention address them.

The last straw occurred one night when I made a house call. It was not a bad area, only a few houses down from the lot where I had once played basketball. I knocked on the door of the darkened basement apartment, and was asked to come in. I cautiously opened the door and turned on the light. Roaches—thousands of them—literally covered the walls. They made a loud scraping sound as they scurried out of sight. Two small children were asleep in orange crates, and their mother, the patient, was in a bed in the adjoining room. I recognized her from high school. She had been smart, she had had potential, but this woman was severely depressed. When I left the apartment I stood on the sidewalk outside, shaken. My legs were weak, my stomach ached. How could this be? In my own hometown? Why?

Nothing in my medical bag was going to solve the problems I saw around me—the roaches, the poverty, the depression. The great amount of family conflict, bad living, anger, and apathy I observed in poor neighborhoods disturbed and confused me. I was not ready for the real world of too many. I had taken my childhood for granted—popcorn and malted milk, happy Sundays, being loved and loving. Mom had used a ruler to break a chocolate bar into four equal parts so that everybody got their fair share. What I was experiencing was not fair.

I needed time to think. I decided that rather than do my military-service time in the Army Reserves, as I had planned, I would do it in the Public Health Service.

Service Time

I served in the Chronic Disease Division of the United States Public Health Service, assigned half of the time to the District of Columbia Health Department, the other half to the Howard University College of Medicine Department of Public Health. I arrived in town with Shirley and our year-old son just before the Fourth of July weekend. American flags were waving and the Spirit of America was in the air.

We drove all over town trying to find a decent apartment, but we were turned away time after time because we were black. Apartments that existed over the telephone were rented just before we arrived. I was the first black officer in the Division. Everybody went out of their way to be helpful. When I asked them about housing they all assured me that there was no problem and gave me all kinds of leads. In those days you didn't embarrass white people with your racial problem. I didn't. The black secretary listened, and when they all left, she came over and gave me the name of a new housing complex where one apartment building had been set aside for blacks. We got a ground-floor apartment next door to a dentist and a city policeman. It was home for the next two years.

At the District of Columbia Health Department I worked part-time in the chronic-disease unit and part-time in the venereal-disease clinic. The patients in the chronic-disease clinic were mostly poor blacks. I noticed that most of them had a second- or third-grade education, if any at all; most of the whites had gone through ninth or tenth grade. The other black doctor there and I called the patients Mr. Clark or Mrs. Williams. The white doctors called women old enough to be their mothers, Sally, Jane, and Mary. None of the doctors wanted to be there. It was income they could count on while building their private practices. One of these doctors had the gall to complain that his tax dollars were being wasted on our lazy patients. I pointed out—tactfully—that he got more of the money than they did.

One afternoon I went to a store in a shopping center serving the area. White blue-collar and government workers lived on one side of the shopping plaza, and a black housing project was across the street. As I drove up, two black youngsters about eleven years old began a fierce fight, and a crowd of mostly white men gathered around to egg them on. I was furious and impulsively jumped in to stop the fight. I leaned down to pick up a pencil I dropped in the melee, and when I stood up the two combatants were standing with bricks aimed at each other. I was in the middle. I had to think fast. I said, "Look, you guys. Do you see all of those white guys standing around trying to get you to fight? They think you're animals. You're not animals. I'll bet you're friends. You don't want to hurt each other. Talk out the problem." The angry scowls gradually left their faces. They dropped their bricks. The crowd dispersed. They had pride. It just hadn't been cultivated. It is the same pride that permits Jesse Jackson to excite an audience of black young people with his chant, "I am somebody."

It was 1961 and white Southern congressmen were on the warpath against the lazy freeloaders on public welfare. I ranted and raved, wrote a letter to the editor of *The Washington Post*, and generally carried on about the nerve of these men, criticizing black people for conditions racial discrimination created; they would not be in office if blacks could vote in the South. They were not legitimate representatives of the people. The hypocrisy infuriated me. And the thing that bothered me most was that many whites appeared to see no evil, hear no evil—and did nothing to stop evil. Didn't anybody care about the lying, the denying! Why wasn't somebody doing something?

It was a question I was soon to ask myself as well.

The Easter Sunday of 1962 I went to brunch with my wife and son at the Bolling Airforce Base Officers Club. The club was plush. My wife was good-looking. My son was bright and handsome. I was a young doctor sitting on top of the world. The meal was delicious. But halfway through, a group of white officers and their wives came in, accompanied by black and white children from the nearby center for displaced children. They ruined my meal. Dad had always said, "Man's highest calling is service to his fellow man." They were helping others. I was doing a lot of talking, but not doing a thing but enjoying my new status and serving me and mine only.

The week before I had heard about an organization called Hospitality House. It was a bootstrap operation— before the days of poverty programs—founded by Nadine Winters, an energetic black woman who is now a District of Columbia councilwoman. A group of middle-income blacks and whites volunteered their services and contributed money to help people who had been thrown off of the welfare rolls for violations of one kind or another, particularly the infamous man-in-the-house ruling. (If a man, any man, was found in the house by a welfare investigator, the women and children lost their welfare payments.) Hospitality House was a modest building in which mothers and their children could stay until they could pull their lives back together and get their own places again. I began to spend as much time there as possible.

I helped people find housing and gave them the support

needed to speak with people at the telephone company, medical clinics, and other services. On one occasion one of the mothers was on the phone with an aggressive telephone company employee who was chewing her out. She burst into tears. I took the phone, told him who I was, and explained that I was a doctor. His attitude changed immediately. Little things do make a difference. Another time I loaned one of the mothers ten dollars until she could get on her feet. When she did, she took great pains to track me down and pay me back.

I enjoyed sitting on the stairs and playing with the children. They were bright-eyed, warm, articulate. I was to learn that this often isn't enough. I stopped by the house one morning and one of the new arrivals was going off to school. He said to his mother, "Where will I find you this evening?" They had been moving from place to place since they were put off the welfare rolls. All of their household goods were on the street in front of Hospitality House. It occurred to me that it must be very difficult to concentrate in school when you don't know where you are going to find your mother in the evening.

There was an open-air market in the neighborhood. In one section a truck would pull up and recruit men for day labor jobs. A white man would stand on the back of the truck and point at this one, that one, and the other one. Black men stood, some with shirts off—sweating, hopeful, resentful, undereducated, trying to get a day's work. I was reminded of pictures of slave sales. It also occurred to me that the children in the house had a good chance of ending up on that day-labor market unless they were successful in school; their chances of being successful weren't good, despite their obvious intelligence.

In the summertime some mothers spent all day in the hot sun taking their kids to two, three different health clinics, sometimes in different parts of town, for conditions that should have been treated in one place that combined all the specialties. They were abused by service personnel, black and white. They were frustrated and depressed. I was beginning to understand the source of the depression I had seen all around me as an intern. Social conditions created mental-health problems. I went out to the National Institute of Mental Health to see what they were doing about the problem. As a result, instead of going back to East Chicago to practice general medicine, I was on my way to the University of Michigan to get a degree in public health.

Reflection and Direction

I arrived at the University of Michigan on August 26, 1963, two days before the March on Washington led by Dr. Martin Luther King, Jr. I had marched in a smaller demonstration the week before and desperately wanted to be in the real thing, but I had to receive our household goods or the delivery date would be pushed back a month. So I sat among crates and boxes stacked in the living room of our new apartment with only the television unpacked. I cheered, pounded on boxes, rolled on the floor in delight, and shouted, "You tell 'em, Martin!" So much that had gone unsaid was being said. For me, like so many other blacks, the March was a powerful day of release and discharge.

It was also a day of confrontation. "What is my role in all of this?" I asked myself. I didn't know yet.

Shirley arrived with Brian several days later. She took one look at our small, barren apartment in a graduate housing center and burst into tears. It wasn't much to look at. But with a little work it wasn't half bad either. We were the only black family in the complex. Shirley, then expecting our second child, asked the black woman who did day work for the couple next door if she would help her a day a week. She explained that she didn't work for colored people.

Overall, however, Ann Arbor would prove to be a haven from racism. It was a good place for our growing Brian. A five-year-old white youngster upstairs explained to Shirley that some people are black people, some brown people, some white people, and all people should be treated the same. He had been carefully taught. Brian, then three years old and the only black child in the neighborhood, mistakenly assumed he was no different, and said he was white. We corrected him calmly and confidently, pointing out that he was black like Mommy and Daddy. That was good enough for him.

The School of Public Health had students from all over the world, which created a stimulating environment. (In later years we visited a Kenyan classmate in Nairobi.) I majored in administration and created a minor in mental health out of available electives. But I was most fascinated with epidemiology and environmental ecology, because I saw the parallels with what would later be called human ecology, the study of how policies and institutions interact with families and children.

It occurred to me that education was becoming critical to a successful adult life. Many kids like my childhood friends and the youngsters at Hospitality House were not receiving the preparation at home necessary to do well in school. And yet I realized that in an open society, it was not possible to intervene at home on a large scale. I began to think of the school as the place to improve the life chances for children from difficult home situations.

I decided that a career in psychiatry would permit me to address social problems. But I was concerned that most psychiatric training programs focused on illness rather than good mental health. Little attention was being paid to the role of social problems in creating mental-health problems. Then I ran across a book by two Yale professors, Fredrick Redlich and August Hollingshead, *Social Class and Mental Illness*. I went to New Haven to interview for the psychiatry-training program at Yale, and was very impressed.

The house officer who escorted me talked about the

problems of poverty. I mentioned race relations and mental health to one of my interviewers, trying to determine how such an interest would "fly" at Yale. He encouraged me to pay great attention to this area. The city itself was in the midst of a major urban-renewal program, one that was to become a model for the country. I could feel the vitality of the city. I felt that my interest in social problems, though not in the mainstream in psychiatry, would be considered legitimate here. I didn't apply anywhere else, deciding that if I was not accepted, I would return to East Chicago after my year in the public-health program and do general practice, or possibly become a local public-health officer.

I didn't go home.

Our second child, Dawn, was born in Michigan in March of 1964. While I waited for Yale, I was on edge. I yelled at Brian unnecessarily one evening. He looked hurt but didn't say a word. He quietly crossed the room and secretly pinched his helpless four-day-old sister who was lying in the crib. It was then that I began to appreciate how primitive and prominent the human feature of scapegoating really is.

President Lyndon Baines Johnson gave the graduation speech that spring. It was a soul-stirring speech in a beautiful outdoor setting:

> "You have the chance never before afforded to any people in any age. You can help build a society where the demand of morality and the needs of the spirit can be realized in the life of the nation.
>
> So, will you join in the battle to give every citizen the full equality which God enjoins and the law requires, whatever his belief, or race, or the color of his skin?
>
> Will you join in the battle to give every citizen an escape from the crushing weight of poverty? . . .
>
> Will you join in the battle to build the Great Society, to prove that our material progress is only the founda-

tion on which we will build a richer life of mind and spirit?"

"I will join," I said to myself, "I will!" It was almost a spiritual experience. In a few minutes the three helicopters carrying the presidential party took off in a dramatic roar, creating great swirls of air and dust, and soared out of sight. I was left with the question, "But what can I do?"

Toward Schools

We arrived in New Haven in the summer of 1964, and the city turned out to be all that my early visit had promised. During my three years of training we lived in a restored townhouse on Court Street, the pride of the redevelopment effort. Each fall the street was closed, and we held a block party to which all the neighbors brought homemade dishes. Each spring there was a cleanup party, more like a coming-out party from the hard Northeast winter. I often had the feeling that this was the way America should be and still could be.

Mom wasn't too happy about my decision to go into psychiatry, but she didn't say so. It was her policy to let us make our own decisions about our future. She had done her job. But she asked me, "What is this psychiatry business all about?" I tried to describe psychotherapy—how you help people think through decisions, become more realistic, confront themselves, and on and on. She listened patiently and then said, "That sounds like common sense to me." I like to think that it's uncommon common sense.

Because I had a great interest in children and social conditions, I was referred to Albert Solnit, then the director of the Child Study Center. Dr. Solnit directed the New Haven Psychiatric Council, a group of experienced psychiatrists working to support the human-renewal effort in the city—programs in housing, child care, education, job train-

200

ing, etc.—called Community Progress, Inc. I was invited to join the council. Through this work I was reintroduced to the needs of the black urban poor.

During elective time I observed and consulted in nursery schools in the Elm Haven Housing Project and the Winchester Elementary School near Yale College. Again I was struck with the ability of so many of the children, in spite of the obvious stress, troublesome behavior, and low academic achievement.

At Winchester I conducted a therapy group for five boys referred because of their aggressive behavior and under-achievement. In short, they fought, kicked, intimidated, couldn't or didn't do their schoolwork, and generally disrupted their classrooms. The home situations of all were similar—no father, an often depressed and overwhelmed mother, inadequate income, generally chaotic home lives. In the therapy group they did a lot of huffing and puffing, but behind it all they were scared kids who wanted and needed adult guidance and approval. After a shaky start the therapy sessions went well.

One day I was in front of my house on Court Street when one of the members of the group, Sanford, happened by. We were surprised to see each other; he was a long way from his neighborhood. We chatted warmly for a few minutes and then my four-year-old son came outdoors. Before I could introduce him, Sanford said, "Is that your son?" When I said yes, he gave Brian a withering look of jealousy, resentment, and anger. It was more than the usual patient-therapist attachment problem. He didn't have a father. He was a handsome and able kid. And it occurred to me that the only difference between him and my son was me.

After two years of training I moved from general to child psychiatry because it was clear to me that so many of the problems of adult patients had their origins in childhood. Also, so much more could be done to prevent future problems with children than with adults. There were so many Sanfords in need.

I had a lot to learn. One hyperactive young patient threatened to throw her paint on me. I was wearing the only good suit that I owned. Seymour Lustman, my professor supervising this case, suggested that I say to her, "You know, if you throw that paint at me, I'll be so angry I won't be able to play with you." I couldn't imagine such a comment affecting the behavior of this uncontrollable youngster. But because I had to save my suit, and my dignity, the next time she raised the paint, I said it. She paused for a second, gradually brought the paint can down, and never tried that again. It was the beginning of my appreciation of the power of the adult-child relationship, as well as the fact that bad behavior is often the way that a child makes a statement of need.

Just before seeing a four-year-old for the first time, his mother told me that perhaps I should have his ears examined first because often he didn't hear her. It turned out that nothing was wrong with his ears. Not hearing was a statement. He was more than a handful for a first-year child resident. He wouldn't go into the therapy room, often pitching a temper tantrum on the stairs as the senior faculty members went by. Once I lost my cool, grabbed him, and carried him into the therapy room. I thought nobody had seen me. But the next day the custodian told me, "That's the way to handle those little brats. You got to show them who's boss. These kids around here get away with murder!" I was ashamed of myself. I had to get consultation, quick.

I was particularly concerned about the rage of the kids who felt that their fathers had deserted them. On one occasion I was tossing a ball with an eight-year-old youngster when I first broached the subject. He fired the ball back at me. Had it not been a whiffle ball, he would have taken my head off—at that it stung. I tried to discuss the same point with another eight-year-old. He stormed out of my office and walked almost a mile through the hospital and back, with me a short distance behind him, before he would say another word. He was angry with me, his father and mother, and himself.

The seeds of a future academic career were being sown. During one of my seminars a professor with a special interest in the family mentioned the black family. When I commented, he asked me to say more and I ended up giving a lecture. My colleagues wanted to hear more, so I gave the next seminar presentation on the black experience and family. Someone suggested that I write an article about it. Me write an article? Nobody in my family had ever written an article before. But I thought about it, and I did. That article was eventually published in *Scientific American*, "The Social Power of the Negro," April 1967, the last year of my training at Yale.

I had made a commitment to become a career officer in the public-health service, though, and hadn't given an academic career any consideration. I returned to Washington in July of that year. The country was in the throes of urban violence by that time. Long-repressed black anger was being unleashed, and not only at whites. On the way to the office I passed a black laborer on a street-construction gang and greeted him, as was the custom, "How you doing?" He glared at me in my suit, tie, attache case, and turned away. I had never had a black person do that to me before.

During the year in Washington I finished my child-psychiatry training by working at the Hillcrest Children's Center in the middle of the inner city. When Martin Luther King was assassinated, the area erupted in violence. On the second day of the rioting I was treating a white youngster, a thirteen-year-old with low intelligence and poor school grades. We discussed his feelings about me and black people in general. He said he had nothing against black people; in fact, he knew that he had to treat them well or they wouldn't want to work for him when he grew

up. Just as he knew his position in life, the black youngsters I worked with knew theirs as well—and no longer
accepted it—one of the reasons for much of the anger and
violence in the street.

A black mailman at the National Institute of Mental
Health barely spoke to me or anybody else on the professional staff, only grunted in response to my greeting. One
Sunday an article expressing my viewpoints on the racial
problem appeared in *The Washington Post*. The next day he
greeted me like we were old friends, now that he knew
where I was coming from. He was a bright guy who was
angry and frustrated by a job market that required more
education than he had.

Soon I was as frustrated with the Institute as he was,
but for different reasons. I sat behind a desk and reviewed
grant applications for projects to help black children sent
in by people who knew very little about the black community's experience. The cities were burning down, and the
government was fiddling with projects that had no chance
to make a difference. Although my colleagues were cordial
and friendly, they were bound by tradition and limited
by the bureaucracy. I called the proposals "assistant professor grants," paying the salary of the professional more
than anything else. My frustration turned to depression
before I received a call from Al Solnit. He told me that he
was submitting a grant to the Ford Foundation to start a
school-intervention project, and he wanted me to come
back to New Haven to direct it. It was like asking a man
dying of thirst if he would consider taking a glass of water.
Here was the chance for me to do my part.

So You Want to Work in Schools?

I wanted to give low-income black children the same chance in life—through education—that I had had. I wanted to find out why the schools were not working for them and to help make them do so. I was delighted to be assigned two elementary schools, Simeon Baldwin and Martin Luther King Jr. All this was fine in theory, but I was totally unprepared for what happened the first day the students arrived. All hell broke loose.

At Baldwin three of the fourteen classrooms were totally out of control. Eight were on the edge and could have fallen apart at any moment. Only the three classrooms with veteran teachers were functioning adequately. I went into one of the classrooms and could not believe my eyes and ears. There were a couple of eight-year-olds chasing each other around the room. Two were standing on tables screaming across the room, imitating something they had seen on television. Other children were whining and crying, "Teacher, teacher." One child was walking aimlessly around the room opening and closing cabinet drawers, dumping paint brushes, pounding erasers, and doing whatever else came to mind with the next thing he encountered. The noise was incredible. Anxious children were sucking their thumbs in an effort to find comfort.

The shaken teacher called for order. The children ignored her. I called for order in my most firm and assertive way. They hesitated a second and then ignored me. That had never happened to me before with children. Mrs. Brown, assistant to the principal for administration, arrived. She was a black woman, a senior teacher, and one of the three people in the project who had been in the school the year before. She knew the children and their parents, and she was able to get them to quiet down. But the problem was far from over. She couldn't stay there and teach.

I retreated to the hallway. One of the children who had been crying followed me out the door. I noticed that he was behind me as I started up the stairs. He was scared and held out his arms. I instinctively embraced him to give comfort, but also to receive it. I was almost as frightened as he was. As he sobbed, his small body trembled against mine. I thought to myself, "Kid, what are we doing to you?"

One part of me said, "What am I doing here?" and wanted to run. The other part of me said, "You want to make a difference—and this is your chance."

It was 1968 and I was director of the Yale Child Study Center team in a collaborative school intervention project with the New Haven school system. Baldwin and King schools were a subsystem in which our team—a social worker, psychologist, special-education teacher—was to develop a way of working that would be applied to the entire school system. We were to work with a principal for administration and a principal for instruction. The strategy was for our team to work in two schools for a year, and then, working with school people and parents, apply our child-development and behavior knowledge to improve the schools.

We were in trouble, I could see that. We adults had to set clear expectations for the children, I decided. I made this point at an emergency meeting of the program leaders. I suggested we hold assemblies and orient the children to these expectations. Everybody was in agreement except the principal for instruction. He felt that this was heavy-handed adult control of children.

A half-dozen teachers expressed the same attitude. Lining up before and after school, walking the children to the toilets, and other order-producing devices were adult conspiracies to repress the young, their spirit, freedom, need for creative expression, and so on. One teacher likened our plans to the abuse of blacks in the South and the Holocaust. I couldn't believe my ears. But it was clear to me that in addition to a difference in concepts about how children develop and learn, a struggle for power was going on.

The principal for instruction was an advocate of open classrooms, a good but often misused concept. Several teachers were his recent students, and several others were interns under his supervision who had not taught before. The open-classrooms approach was described as especially useful for black children—victims of the effects of oppression and abuse passed down from generation to generation for three hundred years. Open classrooms would free them and allow them to benefit from their heretofore repressed intelligence. Teaching was to be lively and exciting—a happening. Learning was to be through exploration and discovery, to be as spontaneous as possible.

In an effort to be cooperative I gave in to the pressure of the principal for instruction. Our views weren't that far apart. I believe that exploration and discovery are important ways children learn, but within a framework of structure. The teachers argued that the problems would go away, that each teacher, not the leadership, had to take responsibility for establishing order. They said that the real problems were administrative: they lacked supplies; some rooms were too large, some too small; some had too many children; and so on.

Most of the teachers were young and white. Excluding the three experienced teachers, the average teaching experience was one year. Three had no previous experience at all. But they were idealistic and enthusiastic. They were out to do better by black people and black children than their parents. They were convinced that black children could do as well as anybody else, and they were going to prove it.

After the emergency meeting the administrators scurried around trying to get the teachers the things they said they needed. Some of the teachers did provide their children with more structure, but most of the open-classroom teachers did not. We soon heard rumors that the parents and the people in the neighborhood were furious and planned to march on the school. That would have destroyed us—a thirty-second television spot, an embarrassed superintendent and central administration, an outraged school board, an angry alderman, and program termination. Wendy Winters, our social worker, was able to talk with a few parents, and I was able to get a community leader to speak with a couple. Instead of marching on the school, they sent a delegation. Boy, were they angry!

There were nine people in the group. They went in to see Mrs. Brown. I heard one person say, "Where is this person from Yale?" Mrs. Brown liked me and tried to protect me, but the parents wanted Yale. Yale had a town-gown problem with all of New Haven, a more serious problem with the black community, and an impossible problem with the low-income black community. In the latter it was known as an institution of great prestige and closed doors. It was believed that its only interest in the low-income neighborhoods around it was to do research. Ironically, the burden of being Yale fell on Hugh and Maggie Comer's son, Jimmy.

When I entered the room, it appeared to me that although the women might have known that I was black, Mr. Best, their leader, had not known. He was a clear-thinking, articulate, forceful man. He stated the parents' concerns directly and succinctly—but with the realization that I was black, some of the anger went out of his voice.

The problem was the usual—promises, promises from the school system and Yale. The schools were to have had experienced teachers, leadership that would give as much time to instruction as to administration, extra money for planning time, participation in program development by parents, and so on. The promises were not kept, and the changes made were not working.

I pointed out to the parents that I had been involved in only a small part of the planning, and that it was my impression that things weren't going well because there hadn't been the kind of planning that was promised. "If you'll give me a chance, it will happen."

They looked at each other and arrived at a consensus without saying a word. Mr. Best turned to me and said, "Okay, we're going to hold you responsible." My being black bought us time, but only "five minutes." They were more interested in results than race.

Now I really had a problem. Within a week of starting, I was being held responsible for making the program work—without official authority or any previous experience in applying the principles of child development and behavior to a school.

Turnaround and Success

W e knew exactly what we had to do to begin. The first thing we did was to invite the parents who came in protest to serve with us on the steering committee for the project. We pulled out the original proposal to the Ford Foundation, reviewed it line by line, and agreed on how to proceed. Genuine trust and cooperation between our Yale group and the parents did not come overnight. It grew step by step, with each problem we addressed and solution we developed together, until it was well established by the third year of the project.

Trust between the Yale group and the school staff developed gradually as well, with a number of ups and downs. Most eventually accepted the need for structure through agreed-on rules and procedures, but the principal for instruction, and one other teacher in particular, did not accept these approaches. And so there was continued strife.

Children were off the desk and the overall sense of chaos was gone within six weeks, but the school climate was not good and the level of learning was very low. It was now a traditional, controlled school, like the one I grew up in, like the one my friends hadn't flourished in, but worse. In my school the principal had been the law and everybody accepted it. In Baldwin School nobody had that kind of authority; order was tenuous—order with a

210

powder keg underneath. The day of the effective authoritarian leader was over.

Our Child Study Center staff and the senior administrative staff of the school made every effort to help the young teachers thrive, but the continued strife between us eventually undermined our efforts to recover with the existing staff. In February we made a decision to try to hold on until the end of the year. We anticipated that some teachers would leave, and if not, we would encourage them to do so.

It was a long time from February until June. The mood of the school during that period could be likened to the long bus trip home of the team who was favored to win the big game but lost. Staff members lashed out at each other. Parents and staff were unhappy with each other. And the children picked up on the strife and reacted by doing numbers on us—fussing, fighting, and so on. Hopelessness pervaded Baldwin School. There were also problems at King, but not to the same extent.

The parents threatened to discontinue the project. I arranged a meeting with Mrs. Hatten, one of the most influential parents at Baldwin School. We talked about our backgrounds, our children, what had been promised to the parents, what hadn't happened and why, as I understood it, and what we needed to do to save the program. Her mood ranged from anger to impatience to empathy. I went to the home of Mrs. Wilkinson, another influential parent, and had a similar conversation. Both agreed that we had to give the project another chance.

When I left Mrs. Wilkinson's house, I stood on the street outside and looked around. Her neighborhood was no different than the one I had grown up in. The parents and children behaved like many of the people I had grown up with. The children seemed as bright as the kids I had grown up with, black and white. There was no reason that they couldn't do well in school.

In the showdown meeting to determine whether we

should continue the project or not, most of the parents, and the superintendent, supported continuation. Most of the open-classroom teachers, even those we wanted to keep, left at the end of the first year. We recruited new teachers in a way so as to achieve a better balance from the standpoint of experience, age, and race. But what was the underlying problem?

I had attended a racially integrated school and had done well, but too many other able black youngsters had not. Most had been from two-parent families. Most people had earned a good living in the steel mills, and so the problem was not simply poverty. Something else was at work. Why was it so difficult for some parents to prepare their children for school, to support them in school, and to give them a reasonable chance in life?

I compared the black experience with immigrant experiences. (Such comparisons are usually a part of the problem because the two are usually viewed as very similar.) The ways in which they differ shed the most light on the educational problem, and other problems, among blacks. If I may digress at some length, let me explain this phenomenon more fully:

Immigrants came into the country largely between 1815 and 1915, most of them after 1865. They were able to maintain a reasonable degree of cultural continuity— language, religion, customs—settling in ethnic enclaves in the new land. This helped them undergo three generations of development that paralleled the three stages of economic change in this country. Many went from uneducated and unskilled in the agricultural and early industrial period prior to 1900, to moderately skilled during the middle industrial period, 1900–1940, to highly educated and highly skilled during the last stage of the industrial era, 1940–1980 and into the post-industrial era. Most heads of households were able to meet their adult responsibilities— caring for self and family, responsible citizenship, and as a result experienced a sense of adequacy, well-being, and belonging.

Immigrants got the vote immediately, and with the co-hesion of cultural continuity used it to acquire mainstream political, economic, and social power. These conditions made it possible for them to improve social and economic conditions for families and their respective groups genera-tion by generation. Opportunities in the mainstream of the society made education important.

This is not to say that immigrants did not have hard-ships, or that some were not overwhelmed by them. Some show the scars of the past today. But most gained during a time when such gains required less education and fewer social skills.

Blacks, on the other hand, experienced severe cultural discontinuity and the social and psychologically damaging effects of slavery. After slavery they were denied the vote through government-sanctioned and quasi-sanctioned ter-ror and subterfuge. These conditions locked ninety per-cent of them into the bottom of the job market—share-croppers, tenant farmers, domestics, the lowest-paid in-dustrial laborers—and to the margins of the society, with-out the political, economic, and social opportunities in the mainstream. Despite this, through the social organization provided by the black church, minimal incomes, and the controls that were a part of small town rural life, most black families functioned reasonably well until the 1950s. In fact, the 1950 census shows that only twenty-two per-cent of all black families were single-parent—now about fifty percent. And black neighborhoods across the country were reasonably safe.

But racist social policies led to massive undereducation of blacks during the period when most Americans were preparing for life in the late and post-industrial eras. In the 1930s, in the eight states that held eighty percent of the black population, four to eight times as much money per person was spent on the education of white children as black, and some twenty-five times in areas that were disproportionately black. The same disparity existed in higher education. As late as the mid 1960s, the endowment of Harvard was more than twice the endowment of the one hundred-plus black colleges combined.

After World War II, education increasingly became the ticket to living-wage jobs, whether the jobs required it or not. Blacks, greatly undereducated, were the first hurt. And without the political and economic power necessary to decrease racist attitudes and employment practices, even the well-educated couldn't enter the primary job market. This is the reason that the black middle class is largely from the professional rather than the business sector, and only recently from the government sector.

Nonetheless, blacks who had experienced better conditions over previous generations eventually produced a critical mass of better-educated people. This led to an intensification of the civil-rights movement and increased opportunities for them. But by the time this occurred, in the mid-1960s, it was already the middle of the last stage of the industrial era. And many families were already experiencing the effects of three generations of exclusion and dislocation—South to North, rural to urban. Many did find a way to survive and thrive under the changed conditions. My family, and my father's family before us, are examples.

At the other end of the spectrum, some black families were traumatized by slavery and the oppressive conditions after slavery, overwhelmed by life in the margins of society. The harmful habits that resulted were transferred from generation to generation. My mother's stepfather is an example. And so are the people who have destroyed housing projects and who are overrepresented in all kinds of crimes and mental disorders.

But most black families are not this seriously disturbed. Most of the children are quite able—like my childhood friends, the children at Hospitality House, and the children we encountered at Baldwin and King schools. On the other hand, their parents have not been a part of the societal mainstream. They often cannot give them the experiences necessary to get off to a good start in school even though they want them to succeed. Some are under economic and social stress, and are unable to do so even when they know what is needed. This was the situation for many of the children at our elementary schools.

American education is structured to serve children who have had the average family experience or better. Teachers are not trained to work with children who have not had such an experience. In the selection of teachers little attention is given to their ability to work with other than mainstream children.

As a result, when children present themselves to the school with behavior that is useful to them on the playground or in a housing project but gets them in trouble in school, they are often viewed as bad rather than underdeveloped, or developed for activities other than school. Without training, the response is to punish the bad behavior rather than to close the developmental gap. Children who have not been read to, helped to learn how to think, express themselves, and don't show good problem-solving competence and confidence are often viewed as slow, with limited academic achievement potential.

Teachers want to be successful professionals. Troublesome behavior and limited intellectual ability are often viewed as obstacles to their professional goals. It is more difficult for school staff to have high expectations for such children. Teachers have difficulty making a positive emotional bond to such children and, in turn, children to such teachers. This makes it difficult for these children to accept the attitudes, values, ways of the school. In fact, these conditions often cause children to feel rejected, to test the staff, to do the opposite of what the staff asks of them—learn and behave appropriately—or just to withdraw emotionally.

My white third-grade teacher held my hand as we walked to school. But because my black friends didn't have the preparation and support to take on the ways of the school—reading library books, in this case—she told them that they shouldn't be in the school. I was hurt and confused, but didn't reject her or learning because my parents, in word and family ethos, told me I could not.

In schools with many underdeveloped children and school staffs unprepared to help, such incidents are more frequent and lead straight downhill for all involved. Parents who had hoped that the school would give their children a better chance than they themselves had, but suspected that it wouldn't, have their worst fears confirmed. They often react angrily, withdraw emotional attachments, or literally stay away. When there are racial, educational, and income differences between home and school, distrust and anger is even more likely. And because the school staff is rarely a natural part of the community, as it was in many places only thirty or forty years ago, the distrust is even greater. All of these factors were at play in the Baldwin and King schools.

One of the reasons that school staffs are ill prepared for children outside of the average expected, or mainstream, experience is that educational reform in the 1930s and 1940s focused on academic standards and content rather than on child development and relationship issues. "Sputnik" in the Fifties, or interest in high technology, exacerbated this problem. All of the educational-reform talk and reports of the past few years ignore child development and relationship issues. And yet when you ask school teachers and administrators what is wrong they say, "A lack of respect, discipline, motivation"—all relationship issues. When you ask high school students why they didn't do well in school, or left, the most often heard complaint is: "The teachers don't care"—a relationship issue. The question I most often hear from school staff about parents is: "How do you get parents to participate in the school program?"—a relationship issue.

At Baldwin-King we had to overcome deep-seated distrust and limited relationship skills among all involved. We created an administrative team for each school that was made up of twelve to fourteen members and headed by the principal. Such a group is still the critical element of our school-improvement approach. Teachers selected by other teachers, parents selected by parents, and representatives of other programs in a school serve on the governance and management team.

Step by step the group identified the most pressing problems and the greatest opportunities, made plans to address them, implemented their plans, assessed the outcomes, and modified the program of the school as indicated. They worked in three areas—social climate, academic, and staff development.

The other important elements of our program were and are the mental-health team, the parents program, and the teaching and curriculum programs. Our mental-health team helped the management group apply child-development knowledge to everything they did in the three program areas. For example, based on our knowledge of child development, we suggested that the kindergarten students enter the assemblies last, make their presentation first, be allowed to listen to the first part of the program, and leave during a break so that they would not tire and become disruptive. This suggestion was based on our knowledge that five-year-olds can only sit and attend for less than an hour.

The mental-health team is made up of a social worker, psychologist, special-education teacher, and any other support staff assigned to a building. In many schools such individuals work individually and, after a child is in trouble, treat the child for a problem. This often causes duplication of services and other difficulties. We discovered one child receiving "services" from seven different people in the school. We worked as a team and focused primarily on prevention.

A transfer student was brought to King School one Monday morning, dropped by his aunt who kept on to work, and taken directly to the classroom by the principal. The teacher had had three transfers the week before and, with a nod of frustration, conveyed rejection to the already anxious child. The youngster took one look at the classroom, panicked, kicked the teacher in the leg, and ran out. Such incidents are often punished by the principal. The child is then sent back to an angry teacher, teased by classmates, fights again, and is sent back to the principal for additional punishment. The process goes around and around until the child is eventually labeled disturbed and sent off to a mental-health person to have his head "fixed."

We had a meeting with the teachers and asked them what they felt it must be like to be eight years of age and to have your entire support system removed. We talked about how it was particularly difficult for this youngster because he was from a rural culture, a town much like the supportive communities before the 1940s. Once the teachers thought about the problem, they developed many ways to support this child and other children in the classroom. Then we thought about how our school as a social system contributed to the problem. A transfer-orientation program was developed that greatly reduced the number of transfer problems.

One traumatized child did not smile at her teacher for eight months. When she did so after trust had developed, the teacher was devastated. She realized that in two more months the child would pass on to another teacher, and she would not be able to build on the relationship. As a result of this concern we considered the problems of discontinuity often present among families moving from place to place, adults moving in and out of the lives of children.

A program of keeping children with the same teacher for two years was developed. Some children who made no academic gain in the first year made as much as two years of academic gain in the second.

Our social worker in particular helped parents work successfully in the school, first as volunteers, then as classroom assistants aiding teachers in academic and social areas. This group of twelve to fourteen classroom assistants formed the core of the parent group. With other parents they developed activities to support the social climate and academic goals of the school. Because what they were doing was important to the school, they urged other parents to turn out. We went from having fifteen to thirty parents turn out for the Christmas Program, say, to having an average of two hundred and fifty.

We worked carefully with parents to make certain that their first projects were successful. Success breeds success and confidence, and as a result they were motivated to participate even more. When parents have a positive relationship with school staff, they can help children accept these people. This is important. When we ask low-income, minority-group children to achieve well in school—an instrument of mainstream society—we are often asking them to be different than their parents. With parents involved, there is no conflict.

When relationships improve in the schools, the children themselves become the carriers of desirable values. At the beginning of the fourth year, someone stepped on the foot of a transfer student and his dukes went up. Another youngster said, "Hey man, we don't do that in this school." He looked at the expressions on the faces around him and read, "We don't fight," and he dropped his dukes. All of these developments reduced the disruption, allowed the staff to have hope and aspirations for the children, as well as to view themselves as good professionals. This gave them the time and energy to focus on the curriculum- and staff-development program.

We tried a curriculum-development program based on individual teacher choices, but it was largely unsuccessful. They needed more guidance and coaching. During the first five years of the project we were not able to get adequate school-system support for curriculum and staff development. As a result, we were never able to make the kind of academic gains that the improved climate, excellent by the third year, would have supported.

The Ford Foundation was prepared to support a dissemination project at the end of the initial five years if the school system had an interest. There was ambivalence. We didn't yet have evidence that our work would raise the academic achievement scores—and scores are everything!

One night while thinking about our future project direction I was having dinner with my wife and children in a restaurant looking out on the Rockefeller Plaza skating rink in New York City. A child of about two was being taught how to skate. His father placed him up on his skates, showed him how to move, and then skated away. The child took a step and fell. The father circled the rink, returned, propped him up, coached him, and skated away again. This was repeated many times; each time the child made a little more progress. Before long he was moving along cautiously without his father, gradually improving. I was aware that many of our students did not have good mainstream social skills. It occurred to me that such skills can be taught when the kind of trust and confidence exists between teacher and pupil that existed between that child and his father.

My siblings and I got along well in school because we had good social skills. We knew when to fight and when not to fight. We knew how to protect our rights in ways other than fighting. But again, we weren't born wise in skills. We were carefully taught and *strongly encouraged* to develop the needed skills and personal controls. We had many opportunities to use them at home, at church, and among friends before our skills were tested and judged in school. When we failed we were given sympathy and encouragement to try again.

This is what happens to most children. But who helps children whose parents themselves have not had such experiences, or who live under such stress that they cannot provide them even when they know what needs to be done? Why not the school?

It was my own family experience, our knowledge of child development, and our experiences in the first five years of the project that led us to focus on social development and social skills. These are things that many educators, parents, and curriculum developers take for granted, or feel have no place in the program of the school because they themselves received such skills and confidence at home.

We argued that the school can and should teach students to present themselves as well-behaved, bright, and able. This in turn would permit the teachers to care about, believe in, and have hope for them. We decided to develop a social-skills curriculum.

In the uncertainty about the future of our project some division developed in the fifth year. Some of the staff and a small group of parents at Baldwin wanted to go back to the more traditional and authoritarian way of doing things. While most did not, rather than divide the loyalties of the school, we decided to leave and to finish out our work in King. We developed the social-skills curriculum at King, and eventually involved another school with low academic achievement, serving a housing project, Brennan Elementary.

The social worker, Carol Schraft, asked the parents at King what they wanted for their children. Not surprisingly, they wanted the same thing for their children that most middle-income parents want for theirs. They were then asked what kinds of experiences and skills their children would need to achieve these goals. Parents and staff decided that there should be four areas of activities in the social-skills curriculum—politics and government, business and economics, health and nutrition, spiritual and leisure time—all areas in which the students would need to be proficient in order to achieve adult expectations. The curriculum was designed to integrate the teaching and learning of basic academic skills, social skills, and artistic expression (a major way of channeling aggressive energy). These units were carried out during what would have been free or elective time so that no time was taken away from the teaching of basic academic skills.

An election for mayor was going on when the first politics-and-government unit was developed. The students wrote letters to the candidates, inviting them to come in and make presentations, and wrote thank-you notes afterward. The parents used money they had raised from bake sales and such to rent buses, and with the staff took the children on study trips around the city. The students were taught how to be hosts for their parents, the candidates, and the staff. They were taught how to raise pointed questions with the candidates, without being disrespectful, so that they would have to answer. The students put on a dance-drama program along with the political presentations made by the three mayoralty candidates.

These activities served to relate the political process to the students in a powerful way. In fact, many of the parents voted for the first time as a result of the experience. It also served to make the basic academic skills more immediately relevant. You must know how to write neatly when you are sending a letter to the mayor! It created a tone that said, "We—parents, teachers, and students—are somebody of worth. Look at what we are doing."

All of the units were designed to create similar outcomes. In each activity the staff worked to help the students gain the kind of social skills which would allow them to interact well. On a study trip to the hospital, the personnel there marveled at the behavior, enthusiasm, and intelligence of these elementary-school children. The kids ate it up and wanted to do even better. An upward spiral of aspiration and achievement was set in motion.

But the acid test was whether the children improved on the Iowa Test of Basic Skills, the standardized achievement test being used by the system. I held my breath the day Carol Schraft walked across the parking lot with the achievement test scores under her arm. When I saw the results in math and reading, the two areas we had targeted for improvement, I jumped for joy and danced around my office. I roared down the stairs to bring the good news to Al Solnit, and we rejoiced together. He had taken a big chance on this project.

The sharp seven-month jump of 1978 was followed by another sharp jump the next year, and the fourth-grade children were scoring at median grade level by 1980. We used the fourth grade as the year of measurement because they were underdeveloped when they came to school, and we expected them to catch up by the fourth grade.

In 1969 King and Baldwin had been thirty-second and thirty-third of thirty-three schools. Recently the children at King have been a year above grade level in reading and mathematics by the fourth grade, and the children at Brennan have been seven months above grade level, third- and fourth-highest levels out of twenty-six elementary schools. The attendance at King has been first and second two of the three previous years, with Brennan edging them out for first during one of those years. There have been no serious behavior problems in King for almost fifteen years, though the children, a large number of them living under stress, come to school with a number of problems and potential problems. There is a similar situation at Brennan.

There was a follow-up study of King students three years after they left the school. In language arts former King students were two years ahead of students from the same neighborhood who attended another elementary school, and more than one year ahead in mathematics. Former King students were also more often student leaders and high-level social achievers as well. The approach is now being used in other low-income New Haven elementary schools, and in elementary schools in several other cities. Middle school and high school projects are now being developed.

Our project, and other projects designed to help low-income children achieve, demonstrate clearly that if we as a nation want to make it possible for low-income black children to achieve at a high academic and social level, it can be done.

All Our Children

Three years ago I was invited to the Martin Luther King Day ceremonies at our original project site, the Martin Luther King Jr. Elementary School. The thirty students in the gospel choir were dressed in white blouses, shirts, and dark pants. They were handsome children, their faces beaming, and they were singing with enthusiasm and excitement. One young lady, Martha, stood out. Among the numbers they sang, "This land is your land, this land is my land." She sang the song with a special gusto, swaying back and forth with an intensity and a sincerity that reminded me of myself forty years before. She had a dream.

Her spirit and desire made me hopeful and apprehensive at the same time. Yes, this land is her land, but it isn't to the degree that it should be for black people. I admire my mother and father and the many black parents who climbed every mountain, forded every stream, who kept on keeping on in the face of race-related obstacles so that their children could have the opportunities available to every other American. But that is no way to run a country.

The unnecessary obstacles blacks faced, and continue to face, means that America loses the skills and contributions of too many. That's what happened with my childhood friends—Nathan English, who died early from alcoholism, Madison Turner, who has been in and out of mental institutions all of his life, and Rudy George, who spent a good part of his life in jail for murder. A trickle make it when it should be a mighty flood.

At the same time, the conditions that made even the trickle possible are eroding. The steel mills that allowed my father to earn a reasonable living are all but silent now—the industrial base of the nation has shrunk. The three-generation movement from uneducated to highly educated that the industrial economy made possible is much more difficult for families and groups to undergo today. Schools, child care, housing, and social-service programs have not been adjusted to make it possible for children and families to function at the level needed in this post-industrial age. What it took to make our two schools work is striking evidence of this problem.

Life in a world changing ever faster because of science and technology is like a relay race with each generation almost desperately passing the baton on to the next. Past and present policies and practices which made it extremely difficult for black Americans to achieve at the level of their ability is like dropping the baton. And black America is not another team in competition with America. Black Americans are a part of America's team. If America keeps running without the baton, no matter how fast or how far, we're going to lose. Black young people with skills and abilities are "all our children." And until they can sing, "This land is my land, this land is your land," and that's a fact, we, America, will not thrive at the level of our potential. Many things must be done to realize our potential. Helping our schools prepare all our children to thrive as adults is one of the most important.

POSTSCRIPT:
Maggie's American Dream

Sometimes when I'm here by myself I get out the scrap-books and picture albums and I just go over everything again. I have yellow clippings about you guys in music, sports, politics, honors—everything. And what makes it nice is that every one of my children have done well. Nobody's leaning on the other one, no backsliders making excuses. You can all take care of yourselves and people respect you for it too. I just look at the way people call on Norman—all of you all—to do things, NAACP, the politicians. And now your children are doing well.

I'm so proud and so thankful. I think back from where I came, I think of all the things that could have happened—this danger ghost hanging over my head—and I get a chill. Sometimes I just pace the floor and say, "Thank you, Jesus." I think of the words of the spiritual, "My soul looks back in wonder, wonder, wonder. How I got over, my Lord?"

I say wonder, but I expected it—I knew. Even as a little barefoot girl back in the country, I had this dream. I had this gift from inside to want something. I thought to my-self that if this one could do it and that one could do it, I could do it. And when I couldn't go on, I said my children would do it. People would say black folks can't do this and can't do that—I wouldn't have any of it. Sure, I could see it was harder for black people, but I just wanted a chance.

227

That's what your father used to say, "Just give my people a chance!"

My only sadness today is that your father is not here to see how well you all have done. He'd rejoice—all of his sons and daughters as professional people. That's what he wanted. That's what we used to sit on the swing on the front porch and talk about and dream about before you all was born even.

Of course, the other thing that makes me sad is that so many of our people have not been as fortunate. Sometimes I sit here and look out the window and see the children playing hookey from school—and far worse things. And I just wish I could tell them and their parents what it takes to have a better life: education. It takes education, especially for our people. That's why I like what you are doing. We've got to try and help our own people.

We can't do it all by ourselves, though.

People say that black folks ought to pull themselves up by their bootstraps. They forget that most black folks didn't get boots, and white folks did. We have to make our own boots, straps and all. With a little more help from the other side, black people would have, you know, respected ourselves more. They would have went to other black people for services and whatever. When we had that little store there in the neighborhood, people came off Carey Street and Drummond Street just to buy from us. It was like a little hidden place, but people would find it because Comer owned it. If people like your dad, Boss Newman, and some of those industrious fellows could have had more for themselves, and there could have been more of them, they could have been a wonderful influence on our people.

Of course, some white people did their share to help. But a whole lot of them tried to stop us every step of the way. I think that's changing now. I hope so. I'd like to see the day when our young people have the same chance that everybody else has. Everybody will be better off, black folks and white folks. That's my dream now.